The Experts Praise
Brand Babble: Sense and Nonsense about Branding

"Don and Heidi have done it again. Here, they deploy all of their worldly wisdom and communication skills in making branding accessible. Practitioners and students will be grateful for their robust approach to a subject that needs to be understood by everyone in business."

TIM AMBLER
Senior Fellow
London Business School

"Finally, a book that points out all of the gibberish being spouted about branding. The Schultzes are candid and insightful, but also entertaining, in clearing the air on this topic. Anyone involved in brand-building should read their book now—before investing another nickel on anything else about branding."

JOE CAPPO
Former Publisher
Advertising Age

"Before investing another dime on brand-related matters, managers and executives should read *Brand Babble*. Don and Heidi cut through the clutter surrounding the brand, often an organization's biggest and least understood asset. Their knowledge about this truly complex subject offers valuable insights on getting the best return on brand equity . . . without wasteful spending."

FRANZISKA DACEK
Vice President
Corporate Communications
Swagelok Company

"Don and Heidi have done a masterful job of cutting through all the clutter and noise to give us a thoughtful, pragmatic and user-friendly look at the branding world as it exists today and—more importantly—how it *should* look tomorrow."

SCOTT DAVIS
Managing Partner
Prophet Brand Strategy
Author of *Brand Asset Management and Building the Brand Driven Business*

"Another great book by Don & Heidi Schultz, which cuts through the 'brand babble' and gets straight to the point. Interesting, insightful and full of useful analogies. A goldmine of helpful information and a *must* for all marketers bookshelves."

DAVID HAIGH
CEO
Brand Finance plc (www.brandfinance.com)

"Any executive who prides him or herself on truly understanding the big picture of how to brand and what there really is to gain from it—or who is building their library for training team members—will want this book."

MARSHA LINDSAY
President & CEO
The Brand Development Firm
Lindsay, Stone & Briggs

"*Brand Babble* is another Don Schultz straight-talking, no-nonsense piece that brilliantly cuts through advertising hype to reveal the common sense of branding. It's full of great examples and solid business propositions. It will ruffle a few feathers as it logically demonstrates that brands must have a meaningful value proposition. If you want to understand brand building, you have to read this book."

PETER SIMON
Senior Partner
Simon Richards Group
Port Melbourne, Victoria
Australia

Brand Babble
Sense and Nonsense About Branding

Don E. Schultz
Agora, Inc.
Northwestern University

Heidi F. Schultz
Agora, Inc.

RACOM
COMMUNICATIONS

THOMSON
™
SOUTH-WESTERN

Australia • Canada • Mexico • Singapore • Spain • United Kingdom • United States

THOMSON

SOUTH-WESTERN

Brand Babble: Sense and Nonsense About Branding
By Don E. Schultz and Heidi F. Schultz

Vice President/ Editorial Director
Jack Calhoun

Vice President/ Editor-in-Chief
Dave Shaut

Acquisition Editor
Steve Momper

Consulting Editor in Marketing
Richard Hagle

Channel Manager, Retail
Chris McNamee

Channel Manager, Professional
Mark Linton

Production Manager
Tricia Matthews Boies

Production Editor
Alan Biondi

Manufacturing Coordinator
Charlene Taylor

Compositor
Sans Serif Inc.

Cover Design
Anne Marie Rekow

Cover Illustration
Lorraine Tuson

Internal Cartoons
© David Metzger

Printer
Phoenix Book Technology
Hagerstown, MD

INTERNATIONAL DIVISION LIST

ASIA (Including India):
Thomson Learning
60 Albert Street, #15-01
Albert Complex
Singapore 189969
Tel 65 336-6411
Fax 65 336-7411

LATIN AMERICA:
Thomson Learning
Seneca 53
Colonia Polanco
11560 Mexico, D.F. Mexico
Tel (525) 281-2906
Fax (525) 281-2656

UK/EUROPE/MIDDLE EAST/ AFRICA:
Thomson Learning
Berkshire House
168-173 High Holborn
London WC1V 7AA
United Kingdom
Tel 44 (0)20 497-1422
Fax 44 (0)20 497-1426

AUSTRALIA/NEW ZEALAND:
Nelson
102 Dodds Street
South Melbourne
Victoria 3205
Australia
Tel 61 (0)3 9685-4111
Fax 61 (0)3 9685-4199

CANADA:
Nelson
1120 Birchmount Road
Toronto, Ontario
Canada M1K 5G4
Tel (416) 752-9100
Fax (416) 752-8102

SPAIN (includes Portugal):
Paraninfo
Calle Magallanes 25
28015 Madrid
España
Tel 34 (0)91 446-3350
Fax 34 (0)91 445-6218

Contents

Preface

Some Rules for Business Books

We have a couple of rules about "business books," this text being of that genre. First, you, as the reader, should ask yourself: Do the authors have any background, knowledge, expertise, history, training, scholarly capabilities, or the like to be writing about the subject of the book. Not just that they have been around a long time, are they qualified? Not every text qualifies on this first rule, although too many readers seem to overlook that fact.

The second rule is, What biases do the authors bring to the subject? Every writer on every subject has biases of some sort. It's important for you, the reader, to know what those are. If you don't, you can often get led down the primrose path of exciting examples, revealing insights, and unreplicable instances that sound really good but are almost impossible to replicate or duplicate. Unfortunately, affiliations or associations with greatness don't help much either. Having carried a CEO's briefcase at one time doesn't make you an expert on how to run a company. So, what *are* the biases or perhaps lack of biases the authors bring to the subject?

The purpose of this Preface is simple: (a) to let you know why we wrote this book and to give you some reasons to think we were qualified to do so; and (b) to tell you our biases up front rather than hide them in catchwords, illustrations, and glittering prose. (The prose that follows is undoubtedly "glittering," but we aren't going to use it as intellectual camouflage.)

So, why did we write this book and are we qualified?

Both of us have spent most of our adult lives involved in brands and branding. Don, on the agency side, started in 1965 and continues to working as a teacher-scholar and global consultant. Heidi initially began as a copywriter for a major insurance company and then worked for a number of years as a key manager at *Advertising Age*, often called the "bible of the advertising industry," and then, later, as a publisher of a major consumer magazine. From a "time-in-service" view, we certainly seem to have some qualifications. But, as we said, having been around a long time doesn't necessarily make you an "authority."

Perhaps more important than longevity, however, is that both of us have extensive classroom and executive training experience through teaching and consulting assignments on brands and branding, marketing, and communication from all over the world. For example, last year, (2002) we taught, held seminars, or had consulting assignment in 17 countries. We've been teaching the "brand equity and brand management" post-graduate course in the Integrated Marketing Communications program at Northwestern University since the early 1990s.

That experience is matched by our writing. Don has been writing a "Brands and Branding" column for *Marketing Management* magazine for the past five years and served as editor of *The Journal of Direct Marketing*. His books—among them, *Strategic Advertising Campaigns* (with Beth Barnes), *Sales Promotion Management* (with William A. Robinson), *Integrated Marketing Communications* (with Tannenbaum, Lauterborn, and Heidi Schultz), *Measuring Brand Communication ROI* (with Jeff Walters), and *Communicating Globally* (with Philip J. Kitchen)—have been best-sellers, still read and used by marketing thought leaders and practitioners everywhere.

So, we've got lots of experience. The question is: Does that qualify us to write about brands and branding, and why would our views be any different or more useful or valuable than the legions of brand experts and brand gurus who have already done so. Again, just doing a "bunch of branding stuff" doesn't necessarily result in brand expertise.

While both of us have extensive experience in advertising and mass communication, we do bring a unique view to the subject of brands and branding. An integrated view—a view that says brands are built, maintained, and generally succeed because of a wide variety of integrated and aligned activities and inputs by the brand owner or maker *and* an equally broad array of things the customer or buyer brings to the encounter with the brand. This integrated view says that makers or manufacturers or developers don't make or build a brand nor do consumers create or develop or conjure up a brand either. It is the combination of the two, the buyer and the seller, working together that is the basis for a successful 21st-century brand. That's one of the things that differentiates this book and its view of brands and branding: the need for integration and alignment of the brand across the marketplace by both buyer and seller.

So, our bias is that there is no "magic bullet" or "magic potion" or "ultimate secret" that can be used to create a brand. It's not one single thing or approach or delivery system that creates branding success no matter what the advertising or public relations or sponsorship or events people say. It's a combination of things, an integrated group of activities and efforts and products and channels and the like, that really are the key to branding success today.

So, our bias is that an integrated approach—not a single element or a single approach or a single ad or a spectacular press release—that builds and maintains a brand. It is the combination and integration of all those elements and more that create and maintain a successful brand. Thus, our bias is toward integration and integrated brand approaches, not toward trying to prove that brands can be built by a particular marketer initiative alone. That's what we think differentiates this book from others.

And, that's one of the reasons this book has been written: our growing irritation with the formula-laden, single-view, advertising-oriented focus on how brands are built and maintained. You'll likely see this starting with page one and finishing somewhere near the end of the text.

The second bias is "instant expertise" and "practitioner qualifications." Too many of today's brand books are based on one person's involvement in, interest in, attachment to, or, simply, proximity to successful brand when it was first started. That historical success is related in breathless prose, intimating all the while that by, copying this "best practice," you can be a successful brand manager or owner or consultant or whatever. Commonly, the success of the particular "brand birth"—detailed and then expanded to the entire universe or, worse still, laid down in a formulaic methodology—suggests instant marketplace success for all those who "follow the rules." Unfortunately, too much of this preaching and sermonizing about brands is based only on "marketplace experience" and little else.

As scholars and academicians, but also as consultants and practitioners, we have small patience for concepts and approaches which have little or no sound grounding or theoretical support. And, we have even less for concepts that distort, adapt, adjust, and sometimes simply mis-use concepts from other areas or disciplines simply because they sound "good" or "solid" or make "cute" or "colorful" soundbites.

We believe marketplace success comes because the brand builder knew the basics of consumer behavior, communication, marketing, sociology, information technology, graphics and design, accounting and finance, and all the other business tools used to create and maintain a major brand presence in today's marketplace. While experience is fine to have, basing one's brand approach on ungrounded concepts and "gut-feel" and "innate instincts" for brand management and brand development are simply too hazardous and expensive for today's marketplace.

Thanks and appreciation on efforts in a text such as this are, and rightfully should be, many. The only problem is that we are certain to leave out some people who contributed greatly to this book.

The influences over a long career are many and the influences over the development of our views are great. Don's came from his early agency days with such brands as Borden Milk, Texas Instruments, Haggar Slacks, Frito-Lay, and a host of others. Heidi's views came from her years at Crain Communications (publisher of *Advertising Age, Business Marketing, Modern Healthcare* and many other magazine titles) and *Chicago* magazine, where she witnessed and learned from hundreds of examples of branding, both good and bad. Together we have learned enormously from heading up best practice studies in branding on behalf of the American Productivity and Quality Center and from our clients who have wrestled with thorny issues of branding, including Hyatt International, CEMEX, Swagelok, Champion International, Technium, and Southern LINC, to mention just a few.

Of particular help in the development of this text, those who are most obvious are Jean Freeman who spent many hours in the library doing academic research identifying the various concepts we felt were important. Debbie Anguizola helped immensely with consolidating some of the chapters and concepts. Brady TenBrink faultlessly handled the manuscript, generally from afar while we were overseas.

Most of all, we are indebted to our publisher of many guises, Rich Hagle. Rich is a long-term associate, friend, and editorial guru who has led us through several publishing ventures. He was the one who brought the Babble concept to us, helped us over the many rough spots along the way, and, most of all, kept assuring us that the project was worthwhile.

So, that's our preface and that's our introduction. On the following pages, we will rail against, poke fun at, challenge and debunk many of today's most treasured brand and branding concepts. We do that because we have found them lacking in solid theoretical support or in mis-guided attempts to provide some type of quasi-scholarly theory for what are too often simply opinions, conjectures, unproved hypotheses, and in some cases simply "smoke and mirrors."

As you'll see, our biases are (a) an integrated approach to brands and branding and (b) the need for solid theory and explication to support brands and branding initiatives. If you understand that, you will understand our reasons for trying to debunk much of what we call "Brand Babble."

Read on and let us know if you agree.

Don and Heidi Schultz
Brisbane, Australia and Evanston, Illinois, USA
September, 2003

1

What Is a Brand?

english is a most imprecise language. Bill Clinton taught us that when he said, "that depends on what 'is' is." That's one reason we have so much trouble with brands and branding. Look at the word "brand." Webster says it can mean any or all of the following:

- A stick or piece of wood partly burned, whether burning or not.
- A sword.
- A mark put upon criminals with a hot iron.
- A mark made by burning with a hot iron, hence, any mark of infamy, a stigma.
- (a) A mark made by burning with a hot iron, as upon an animal to designate ownership, or upon a container to designate the quality, manufacture, etc., of the contents; (b) a similar identifying mark made in any other way, as a trademark, hence, quality, grade class, or make of goods as a good brand of flour.
- An iron used for branding.

Not much there to confirm or deny how the term is used in marketing in the twenty-first century.

So, what is a "brand" and what is "branding"?

The brand babblers have it figured out. It's like Humpty Dumpty: "It means just what I choose it to mean, neither more nor less."[1] It's this lack of agreement that causes much of the confusion, lost motion, wasted efforts, and misplaced investments in brands and branding today.

And a lot of brand babble to boot!

But there's plenty more to add to the confusion. The marketplace is filled with self-proclaimed "brand experts," "brand consultants," "brand gurus," and, yes, even academics parading as brand authorities. All using their hocus-pocus models, diagrams, geometric shapes, and clever analogies to explain what most of us have trouble verbalizing.

That's what this book is all about.

Breaking through the clutter . . . the confusion . . . the contradictions. In short, the brand babble that is inundating the marketplace today.

Our call is for clarity. Clear-headed thinking. Rational approaches and most of all, a business-like approach to the subject.

In our view, it's time for some relevant discussions on how brands are used, how they can benefit the organization, how they can be understood as intangible assets for the firm. But, most of all, why and how organizations can use brands to make money.

That's right. This is a book about making money. Making money with brands and branding. Investments and returns. Short and long-term profits. Shareholder value. All the things that drive businesses today.

So, what you'll find in this book are some proven and provable facts about brands. Brought to you by two people who are willing to poke holes in the inflated hyperbole and challenge all the prattle about brands and branding that engulf most marketing departments and is quickly seeping into management suites as well.

What we plan to do in this book is to talk about brands as a way for an organization to make money. Now and into the future. Call it "Value-Based," "Economic Branding," or whatever. We're going to be shameless about looking at brands in a hard-nosed-business way. You'll find none of the namby-pamby brand prattle here. We'll cut through the babble to help you understand what is "really" being said. All you'll find is a clear, concise, and maybe a bit cynical, view of brands and branding. But, that's the only way we think you, as a manager or owner, can cut through the clutter and babble that have grown up around these very valuable assets called brands.

So, if you're not interested in making money with your brand or brands, put this book away. Keep doing what you've been doing and be prepared to sink a bunch of money in a batch of myths, opinions, hopes, and dreams that likely won't ever pay out.

Brand Babble

Let's start with the title: Brand Babble.

Webster defines babble as:

"To talk as a little child or idiot, indistinctly, meaninglessly or incoherently." Sounds a lot like today's brand advice doesn't it?

So, the view is that the marketplace is filled with brand babble—multiple views, multiple voices, multiple concepts, and multiple authorities. Everyone shouting and no one making much, if any, sense.

Today, branding is much like the biblical Tower of Babel in ancient Babylonia, where King Nebuchadnezzar gathered numerous tribes, clans and cultures. Great idea. Get all the best minds in the world together. The problem: No one could understand anyone else. Everyone with his or her own thoughts, ideas, concepts. Everyone talking. Nobody listening simply because there was no clear theme or concept or even language that could be used.

That's branding today.

Conversations about brands and branding are so steeped in so much mythology, terminology, and pseudo expertise that few marketing people and even fewer senior managers can make any sense out of the babble. And that's a problem.

For most organizations, the brand is the most important asset they own . . . free and clear. And, commonly, it is one of the most mis-managed.

Why?

The graphic above illustrates the problem. Multiple experts, shouting a myriad of complicated, complex messages with confused or conflicting meaning and less clarity than the Mississippi River.

In Nebuchadnezzar's time, the Tower of Babel had only one location. And, the babble could reach only as far as the human voice. Today, with the development of electronic communication,

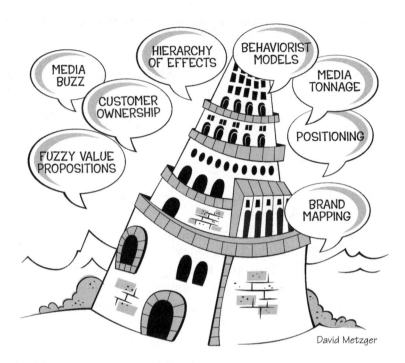

David Metzger

Branding's Tower of Babel

the ability of the brand babblers to distribute and proselytize un-proven views and undefined theories on brands and branding be-come almost too easy. The result: We're literally swimming in a sea of brand bravado.

Just look at the brand babbling. "Brands are animals." "Brands are consumer badges." "Brands are trademarks and trade dress." "Brands are advertising." Or, "Brands are boxes and bags and logos." "Brands are positioning." Or a dozen other terms and concepts.

Lots of babbling about the brand and branding but little dis-cussion about brands as corporate assets . . . as future income flows . . . as entities in which the firm can invest and make profits.

Why is there so much of this brand babbling? If you don't know what you're trying to do with your brand and brand program, most any of the multitude of brand approaches will get you there. So, maybe all the babble is useful to the uninitiated and the mis-directed.

For the rest of you who are really trying to make sense out of all this brand babble, to lead your organization toward marketplace success, some clear thoughts and some rational explanations will probably help.

A Clarion View of Brands and Branding

So, the first step in breaking through the brand babble is to define what is meant when the magic word "brand" is used in this text. Are we talking about a logo or icon? About the product or service? About the advertising? Or the trade dress and the logotypes?

Or do we mean the physical properties? Or the characters and representatives? Or the attitudinal relationships? Or maybe the images and concepts that represent value? In short, what do we mean by "brand"? Unless and until that is done, i.e., what we'll be discussing is verbally described and differentiated, we'll continue to drift in the sea of babble about brands and branding.

Sometimes the best definition of a term comes by saying what the thing isn't. In spite of what many self-proclaimed brand experts say, a brand is not a magic elixir. It's not something that will rescue a flawed business concept, as most of the dot.coms learned to their chagrin. It's also not something that can be created out of whole cloth and foisted on an unsuspecting public. And, it's certainly not a neato-jet product with a jazzy set of graphics. And, most of all, the brand is not something that is "created" through an endless series of expensively produced television commercials, no matter how clever the concept or how many industry awards the spot wins in Cannes.

Further, a brand is not a mental model. It's not something that can be fully explained through a four-box matrix. Nor is it a spreadsheet that estimates Net Present Value or Discounted Cash Flow going out to a terminal value. In truth, a brand is partially all of those things and, quite literally, none of them totally.

Again, in our view, the brand is simply a way for the brand owner to make money. Pure and simple. An economic tool that provides value for its owner and also value for its buyer.

A brand, simply put, can exist on many levels and in several dimensions. Sometimes it's an inanimate hunk of metal sold by a group of dedicated machinists. Sometimes, it is a simple sheet of paper with some sticky on the back that can be repositioned. Other times, it's the relationship between an 18-year-old and his boom box. Or, sometimes the brand is a way of life or a culture. So, in our view . . .

The brand can be a product.

Or a service.

Or a person.

Or a thing.

Or an idea.

Or a process.

Or a country.

Or an organization.

Or almost anything.

In short, a brand is something that both the buyer and the seller can identify and for which some type of exchange agreement results in the creation of value for both parties.

So, that's what we mean by a brand: something that is identifiable by the buyer and the seller and creates value for both.

To make sure there is no misunderstanding, the brand is technically a legal entity that can be bought and sold and re-sold. And the owner of a brand can change as quickly as a contract can be drawn. This legal definition of a brand is important, for it entitles the brand owner to profit from the brand. And, that's a key point. Brands are supposed to make money for the brand owner. If they don't, why have them and why own them?

Do You Need a Sack of Money to Build a Brand?

Much of the babbling about brands and branding centers on money, that is, spending by the brand owner. One of the first things most pseudo-brand experts say is "branding is expensive." "Brands cost a lot of money." "If you can't support a brand with tons of advertising, you can't build a brand."

All that is hogwash.

Brands shouldn't cost money. Brands should make money. Why would any organization invest a ton of money in something that isn't going to produce a big return? That's what governments do, not practical businesses.

Yet, look at all the babble about the cost of branding.

For example, in several recent issues of *Advertising Age*, the bible of the advertising industry, it was reported that Kia and Infiniti would be spending $40 million each to launch their new SUV sub-brands, (Note: These are "sub-brands." Wonder what a "first-floor brand" brand would cost?).

About the same time, Cisco announced a $150 million effort to restore some luster to its hot high-tech brand image.[2]

Those are big bucks in any league—almost enough to rent your own NBA player for a couple of weeks.

Branding, the way it is practiced today, is expensive. And, that's the issue: Brands shouldn't cost; they should pay back.

For years the so-called branding experts have passed around an industry rule–of–thumb that it takes between $20 and $50 million to launch a new grocery store brand. And, if you have a margin of 20% on a 50-cent item, it's going to take you a long time to get those multi-millions spent on brand spending back.

The shortcoming of most "rules-of-thumb" about brands and branding, though, is that *no one really knows* what it costs to build a brand.

Even more frightening is the supposed cost to maintain a brand. For example, according to *Brandweek*, in 2001, McDonald's reportedly spent $629 million on media to maintain and build their brand.[3] Yet, between 2001 and 2003, McDonald's sales, share and profits continued to erode. McDonald's spent a lot. Doesn't look like they got a lot back. What's wrong with this picture?

Spending big bucks on a brand doesn't mean the firm can stave off major organizational problems or social evolutions as McDonald's is apparently learning.

The problem with all these glorified "reports on brand spending" is simple. All they really tell us is what some one or some firm spent on behalf of a brand. It says nothing about how much they got back in return.

And that's the key point of this book. It's not how much you spend on a brand; it's what you get back that really counts. Few of the branding gurus or brand consulting mavens ever discuss brand returns. Yet, that is the most important reason for owning a brand: to generate future income flows, not to provide a siphon for current profits.

Can You Build a Brand Without Media Spending?

In the beginning, The Body Shop spent little on traditional marketing communication to build their brand. Starbucks followed much the same path. And, in the beginning, even Dell didn't invest heavily in traditional media advertising.

So, the answer to the question is: Yes, you can build a brand without big media investments. There are hundreds of successful companies and thousands of successful brands that have used a wide variety of methods to develop and maintain a successful brand.

The problem with looking at what others spent or spend on brand advertising and other media forms in developing their brand is the numbers are meaningless. No one knows what it costs to build a brand. In fact, the question is immaterial. The real questions revolve not around spending but around building, growing, and getting returns.

The first real challenge in brand building is not how much you can spend. It's "What's the basic value you are going to offer prospective customers?" The next question is: " In what form or format are you going to present your offer so that prospective customers can give you money to get it?" Then, and only then, do you come to the question of "How are you going to communicate that specific value to the specific groups of people who need or want that value?" And big advertising spends aren't always the answer.

So, the basic problem with most brand babble today is that the gurus start with how much you, as the brand owner, should spend, not with how much you'll get back. Even the most wet-behind-the-ears brand manager can spend money. The key skill is getting a return.

So, if you want to determine whether you're talking to a brand babbler or a brand builder, see where they start the conversation. With spending or returns.

Sometimes You Can Just Wander into a Brand

Some of the strongest brands around today didn't have a lot of spending of any kind behind them in the beginning. They simply grew like the fabled doll, Topsy. The owners or managers or promoters initially set out to sell a product or service they either made or acquired. In the course of selling the products, the brand sort of emerged. No four-box matrices. No plumbing the depths of human consciousness. No whiz-bang computer models. L.L. Bean didn't set out to build a brand; he set out to sell his high-quality outdoor wear. The L.L. Bean brand just happened along the way. Henry Ford didn't set out to build a brand. He just wanted to make cheap cars and sell them to people. Monet and Renoir didn't set out to invent the "Impressionist" school of painting. They just wanted to paint what they saw. And, if memory serves, they made little on the paintings. It was the later owners who really generated all the value and returns.

So, no, it doesn't necessarily take a sack of money to build a brand, but it does take a sack of understanding to know when you have invented . . . or perhaps "created" . . . or maybe just stumbled onto brand. And, of course, the key element is what to do with it once the brand exists.

You Don't Really Know What a Brand Is Worth until Someone Buys It from You

The real value of a brand is not what you spend to build it, it's what you get back from having done so. There are lots of ways to do that.

The brand babblers expound that the only real way to determine the value of your brand is to see how much more the customer will pay you for your product with the brand than a like product without the brand. Of course, that's a little hard to do since your brand has your brand on it and taking it off makes little economic sense. So, one of the key elements in branding is creating value. And, it doesn't have to be just a price premium over competition. It's whether or not you make money by selling the brand. Remember, Wal-Mart grew to be the 800-pound gorilla of the retailing world, not by charging more, but by charging less.

The Acid Test of Brand Value

In truth, and in spite of all of today's financial gimmickry, the only way to determine the financial value of your brand is to sell it to someone else. No, we don't mean sell the products or services that make up the brand. We mean physically transfer all the brand ownership and accoutrements to another person or company.

Find out what they will pay you to own your brand. Until then, anything and everything and every figure you will see or that can be hypothesized about the value of your brand is just a guess. Until someone plunks down cash on the barrelhead, everything is just speculation.

Now, we grant, some of the guesses can be fairly close but that only counts in horseshoes. Unfortunately, too many are way off. So, the value of your brand is what someone else is willing to pay you for it. In cash.

Of course, here we're referring to a potential owner who understands the marketplace, sees the potential in your brand, and has the resources to offer you fair market value. None of those clever earn-outs or nifty stock ownership transfers. The brand is worth what it will bring in cash. Nail that on the door and look at it every time you pass by.

What a Brand Can and Can't Do for an Organization

The final point in this first chapter is what a brand can and can't do for you and your firm.

Brands can . . .

- ◉ Create financial value for the owner in both the short and long term.
- ◉ Create various forms of value for customers so they are willing to seek out the brand, buy it and continue buying it.
- ◉ Create relationships with employees and other interested stakeholders so they want to continue to be associated with and support the brand.
- ◉ Last a long time or at least be remembered a long time. That means long-term income flows.
- ◉ Become a part of the culture. Cultural icons have great value. Just look at the value Michael Jordan created during his basketball career for both himself and those he worked with and for.

But, brands can't . . .

⊙ Belong, in the mental sense of ownership, to any one or any firm. Everyone "owns" a piece of the brand. But, brand owners get first claim on the financial returns.

⊙ Rescue a bad business model or a poor product or service.

⊙ Overcome a destructive reputation or unethical business practice.

⊙ Make enough to pay a dividend to the owners or managers forever. Brands sometimes fade and die like everything else, even with the best management.

⊙ Be managed the way you run a factory or operate a garbage disposal.

In short, brands are one of the most complex of any business activity. They're also one of the most of the durable, yet one of the most fragile, of all business assets. Brands are not intuitive. They aren't something the CEO's spouse can learn about at the mahjong table and therefore give unlimited guidance. Brands are as important as you make them and as useless as you mismanage them.

But, one thing is for sure. Brands are supposed to make money for the owner. If your brand is not making money for you, you've probably gotten too deep into the brand babble.

Brands are complex. That's true. It's this complexity that engenders all the brand babble. And, it's why there are so many brand experts running up and down the aisles of companies around the world. And, why many of them should be tripped, trapped, and put away.

The real purpose of this book? To help you, as the brand owner or brand manager, sort through all the branding mania that exists and come to grips with how to really think about, manage, and make a profit from your brand or brands. Anything else will be a waste of both your time and ours.

Notes

1. Lewis Carroll, "Alice Through The Looking Glass."
2. *Advertising Age*, March 10, 2003, February 3, 2003, and February 24, 2003 editions respectively.
3. *Brandweek* SuperBrands Issue, June 17, 2002.

2

Who Owns the Brand?

$\mathfrak{A}$t first blush, that sounds like a pretty dumb title for a chapter in a book on brands and branding. Particularly when we announced in Chapter 1 that this book was about how the brand owner could derive economic benefit from the brand.

Of course, the answer to the question is the person or group who has a legal right to the brand returns.

But, there is a second view that is important to understand, too.

Today, in many brand guru lairs, it has become fashionable to pronounce, "The customer owns the brand." But, in other dens of brand expertise, you'll hear, "The company owns the brand and has the right—yea, even the responsibility—to grow it, extend it, optimize, and exploit it as much as possible."

This brand ownership debate is a meaningless discussion. It's just more brand babble that diverts understanding from some very fundamental brand truths.

Brands, in all their intangible glory in the marketplace, really represent relationships. They connect the organization to the customer and vice versa. To debate who "owns" the brand is to muddle concepts of ownership and equity and to miss the real point about how brands create value for both sides. While we focus primarily on the economic value of the brand to the owner or marketer in this text, we recognize the inherent value and relationship a brand must have with a customer for it to be successful. But, given our focus, we may take what some would consider an extreme view.

The Law Decides

This "dual nature" of brands is clear in the laws that have evolved around them. In advanced economies, trademark and copyright laws recognize the marketplace value of a brand and the rights of the owner. Thus, laws try to protect brand owners from counterfeiting, forgery, or other unauthorized use.

At the same time, the laws also protect buyers against the foisting off of fraudulent goods and attempt to assure buyers and users of the consistency, quality, and origin of the brands they purchase.

So, maybe there is some reason for lawyers after all.

The question of "who owns the brand" masks another issue. That has to do with whose view of the brand is being promoted. Is the brand what the company says it is? Or is it what customers believe or think it to be? Is one view more "true" than the other? The babblers would have you think so because to them, most everything about a brand is black and white, either-or. Whatever supports some magic brand formula.

In the most literal, legalistic sense, brands are owned by the company holding the trademark. As owners, they can sell the brand in its entirety, just as Bristol-Myers Squibb did to gain $4.95 billion when it sold the Clairol brand to Procter & Gamble in 2001. Or they can "rent" it to another company, just as Starbucks did when they licensed their name to Dreyer's to produce a premium line of coffee-flavored ice cream and likely received some type of payment in return for that use.

Can Brand Owners Do Anything They Want?

But, problems sometimes occur with brand ownership. That happens when brand managers falsely believe that, as the surrogate brand owners, they can do anything they want with the brand; i.e., extend, leverage, stretch, and otherwise push, pull, and twist the brand to the point it is no longer recognizable or useful to the buyer.

David Metzger

Who really *"owns" the Brand?*

Marketing history is full of such brand owner/manager arrogance and ignorance. What else can explain such branding blunders as the Nova from Chevrolet. Nova means "doesn't go" in Spanish—a major problem for an automobile. Or, new Coke or Harley Davidson wine coolers or Bic perfumes.

Brands have expansion possibilities, but they can only go so far.

The idea that the customer owns the brand partially evolved from these types of unilateral and arrogant brand owner/manager actions. But, "customer ownership of the brand" has limitations, too—especially when considered in contemporary marketing terms. A brief jaunt back into history will help explain why many brand experts are so wrong today about brand ownership.

In the Beginning . . .

Back in the early 1930s and 1940s, when the boys in Cincinnati (read Procter & Gamble here) and the guys who shared time between London and Amsterdam (insert Unilever here) were developing the first stages of formalized, 20th-century branding, it was much easier to create a brand from scratch.

The products being sold were primarily mass-produced, volume-driven household products. Things the consumer generally had only dreamed about, but had never experienced . . . dishwashing soaps, washing detergents, bar soaps with colors and smells, window cleaners, scrubbing bubbles, margarine that tasted good, and so on.

The package goods people (sometimes referred to as 'fmcg'— fast-moving consumer-goods) quickly learned to talk "product benefits," not "product attributes," to prospective customers to extract more returns. Thus, they created dreams and fantasies for consumers, mostly through mass media advertising. If you're over 40, you likely remember the Breck Girl, the Keebler Elves, Mr. Clean, or Charlie the Tuna.

Branding worked in those days, because the marketing organization controlled the system, i.e., everything about the product, the brand, and the marketplace. Young product managers in Cincinnati and their ilk in Minneapolis, White Plains, London, and other marketing centers, determined what would be put in the box or bottle based on their design. They determined the price, the channels, and, most of all, they controlled the communication describing the product and the associated dreams and rewards it could or would or should provide. The marketer created the brand, then transferred those ingredients and images to the customer through communication, primarily through the exciting new medium of television.

Customers took in the brand imagery, bought and used the product. That allowed them to relate it to their own experiences, perceptions, desires, and needs. Thus, a brand was born. The brand manager was the guide, and the consumers were the followers and, in some cases, they even became the brand apostles and disciples.

The brand transported the purchaser into the magic land of success and happiness and adoration. The success as a mother, as a wife, as a homemaker—came from happiness that came in a box or bottle. Plus, the adoration that came from a loving family and spouse.

Or, alternatively, the man was transported to the land of ongoing business success simply because he smoked the right cigarette, wore the right hat, or drank the right whiskey. That's what dreams are made of, and that's what marketers were selling.

Savvy marketers extended their impact by giving unique identities to their brands, often based on products with few, if any, distinctive physical attributes. Thus, P&G was able to introduce Tide, Cheer, and Oxydol, each with a distinctive brand identity and perceived purpose, in the same product category through the magic of mass media advertising.

This same brand magic worked in other categories as well. For example, cosmetics companies supported brand lines ranging from the high-end department store variety to those found in drug stores and supermarkets. Even today women would be shocked to know how little product difference there is between the $25.00 department store eye shadow and one sold for $4.00 in the local mass merchandiser. But, the brand owner sure knows. Big bucks.

So, yes, there's an element of truth in the "customer owns the brand" argument because the customer creates his or her own dream world where the product and the brand makes their aspirations possible. But, the customer can only own so much of the brand. Certainly not the financial value. That clearly belongs to the brand owner.

When Dreams Went Wrong

Marketers today have much less latitude in creating a brand. While there is still the possibility of dream-making through advertising, the marketplace is radically different, as is the consumer. Today, there are simply too many competitive consumer choices. Too many alternatives. Too many things to buy, ways to buy, methods to buy and ways to experience. In short, too much marketing and too much communication make branding a totally different game in the 21st century.

This excess has changed the nature of the marketplace and how a brand is built and maintained. Today, the consumer doesn't want to "own" the brand. That's too much of a commitment. They just want to "borrow" the brand, use it, and then, in many cases, trade it off for something else. Or, at worse, return it to the marketer for another model. That's why, if you, as the brand owner, don't understand the 21st-century process, you could spend millions and end up with a handful of recycled rejects.

An Even Bigger Change

People. Today, marketers can still control the products they make. But, it's much more difficult to control the people who deliver the customer brand in the myriad ways customer's buy. Whether it's the barrista serving up a latté, a technical support expert resolving a software problem, or a bank teller selling traveler's checks, brands today are indelibly shaped by the people employed to interact with customers. It's this "people-thing" that many brand babblers don't recognize or account for in their charts, graphs, consumer projections, and conceptual hocus-pocus.

Branding for people-based organizations, such as banks, airlines, hotels, and many b-to-b marketers, is fundamentally different than the model perfected by the packaged goods guys. Yet, because the fmcgs had the first success and developed the first brand model, everyone began to believe that was the way branding was done. And, of course, the refugees from the fmcgs, who became the prime brand babblers, picked up on that theme. In too many cases, it seems they have extended and expanded it beyond even what the most enthusiastic detergent manager ever considered.

The Proof Is in the Web

In the 1980s and 1990s, when the technology boom broke, every business concept ever devised in an MBA course flooded the market. Interactivity was going to rout the "old economy bricks and mortar" sellers. Brands were the thing. Build a brand and become a billionaire.

And, brand building was easy, said the babblers. Develop some neat graphics. Computer-generate some "breakthrough" creative. Lots of media money, with the more bizarre the media the better and the more bizarre the creative concept obviously driving the entire approach.

Unfortunately, all that brand building was based on the tired old concepts of product branding the fmcg-guys had done 40 years earlier. So, every "new economy" marketer hurried to emulate the strategies of P&G, Unilever, or Colgate, at times even hiring "brand managers" from these temples of branding wisdom.

These fmcg wannabes set the tone for the dot.com boom and bust. Selling products on-line, with their high service requirements, just didn't work. It wasn't like selling Hellman's Mayonnaise or Dr. Gramont's Yogurt or a bottle of Windex off the shelves of Safeway.

People, not just advertising, made a big difference in dot.com branding. Today, the marketing scene is radically different. Moving from a product-dominated marketplace to one that is increasingly reliant on services has changed the entire approach to branding—dramatically. The problem is: The babblers haven't caught onto this so they keep pushing the same old Cincinnati models as if it's still in the 1950s.

That's where most branding gurus, experts, and pundits fall short. They try to take time-worn fmcg approaches—as if it's still the mid-20th century—and apply them willy-nilly to every branding situation for every type of company around the world. One model. One approach. One system. In spite of the fact that the products are different, the market is different, the consumers are different, the media is different. In short, they're pushing applications for concepts that are no longer relevant. That's why so many of them fail, so often. But, the brander only knows this once the money has been spent.

The Heart of the Matter: The Brand Starts Inside

Today, there's no question about what's important if you want to make money in branding. In a people-dominated marketplace, the brand starts inside and radiates outward. It doesn't start with nifty external concepts and work back in.

Today, in any customer-facing organization, it's the people inside who deliver the brand experience that make the difference. It's those "non-brand-trained marketers," aka employees, who drive brand sales and profits. Their commitment and the experiences they deliver to customers shape and deliver the brand, and it is only through that commitment and those experiences that success occurs. These internal folk give the brand the character, personality, and distinctive quality that make it unique. They are the ones who typically keep customers coming back for more, at least as much, and often more than the product itself.

So, today, your brand's personality is more often defined by how real, living, breathing employees serve customers, not by some ad agency creative team trying to create a fictional "Never-Never" land.

This brand personality may be warm and welcoming (Starbucks), efficiently professional (Ritz Carlton), or funny and a bit raucous (Southwest). But it reflects the heart of your organization: who you are, how you think, how you act. The brand is the people who make up and define your corporate culture and your brand.

So, if your company can deliver on the right brand experience consistently, and customers and prospects find that appealing, then the brand will grow and prosper and you will continually put money in the bank.

If, however, your company and your brand have no heart, no soul, or no personality that define it and provide cohesion and energy for your employees, the brand will be the same way. Bland, feeble, and far more subject to pricing pressure, customer churn, and declining margins.

So, let's cut through the babble: The brand starts inside, with its people and their commitment and enthusiasm, not with ingredients and gimmicks and made-up characters. The brand starts inside and radiates out. It doesn't start with the customer and come back in. That's why the "consumer owns the brand" experts have so much trouble helping organizations. They continually look outside when the brand answers are right under their noses.

But, remember, no consultant can charge very much to say, look at your employees. Ask them. Yet, in case after case, we've found the brand is what the people who deliver it are. That's how you make money with branding. You start inside, not outside.

Surprise! There Is No Surprise.

The preceding is not really a breakthrough idea, although you would think it was, given the surprise it brings to brand managers accustomed to thinking first about a television commercial and practically never about a line worker. Yet, Avis recognized this years ago with its "We Try Harder" theme. Today, Starbucks lives off their barristas. Dell lives off their teleservice people. Southwest lives off their flight attendants. Nordstrom lives off their helpful sales clerks. Those are elements competitors can try to copy but can never own. Those are ingredients that belong to your brand and to your brand alone. And, those are the things you need to manage to make money on your brand.

Complications Set In

The brand management challenge is, of course, people aren't consistent. It's not like making and distributing a box of Cheer or a package of Kraft cheese. People aren't infallible like the formula for a bottle of Heinz Catsup. And they certainly aren't as predictable as the taste of Coca-Cola. The inclusion of people in the branding business makes the development of all brands, and especially service brands, incredibly more difficult than their fmcg counterparts. The simple truth: Today, branding must start with employees, channels, distributors, wholesalers, suppliers and work its way out. The brand is what the company is. Nothing more. Nothing less. If the folks who deliver the brand experience aren't sold on the brand and don't "live the brand," why expect a customer to do so?

A De-Babbler Process: Getting to the Heart of the Brand

At the risk of sounding like another "babbler," we're going to put forward one approach to brand understanding that works.

Below, you'll find a process called "Getting to the Heart of the Brand." That simply means understanding what the brand means or can mean to all of the key stakeholders. The process isn't that complex. In fact, it's similar to what many brand consultants call a "brand audit," but, it's a brand audit with a different view. It's a view of the inside, not just outside.

Note: This process relies on inputs, but not just inputs from customers and prospects, important as they may be. "The Heart of the Brand" is how the key stakeholders feel, especially those who touch customers on a regular basis. It engages rank-and-file employees to determine what they believe and what they are capable and willing to deliver as the brand experience. And, that's what the brand really is, the experience the customer receives time after time, day after day, in good times and in bad from everyone who represents the brand.

That's "The Heart of the Brand": what employees and other customer-facing stakeholders believe the brand is and what they can and are willing to deliver to customers on an ongoing basis.

Unlike most brand babblers, we aren't going to give you chapter and verse on how to use "The Heart of the Brand" approach.

Exhibit 2.1

GETTING TO THE HEART OF THE BRAND
A Process

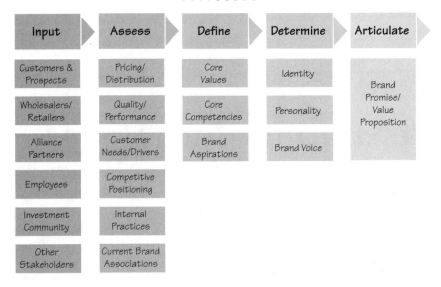

Input	Assess	Define	Determine	Articulate
Customers & Prospects	Pricing/ Distribution	Core Values	Identity	Brand Promise/ Value Proposition
Wholesalers/ Retailers	Quality/ Performance	Core Competencies	Personality	
Alliance Partners	Customer Needs/Drivers	Brand Aspirations	Brand Voice	
Employees	Competitive Positioning			
Investment Community	Internal Practices			
Other Stakeholders	Current Brand Associations			

That's fairly self-evident. The only thing we will suggest is that the key to the brand is found under the heading "Define." There you'll find three elements: "Core Values," "Core Competencies," and "Brand Aspirations." Those are what the employees and other internal stakeholders must define and accept, not something that can be dreamed up in a boardroom or rolled out of a creative department. It's what the organization really is and what its people can really deliver.

So, Who Owns the Brand?

The answer is simple. Of course, the owners own the brand, but the employees and stakeholders contribute to the well-being of the brand, too. And, the customer who reaches into his or her pocket or wallet or purse to buy the brand has a form of ownership in the brand as well. Each plays a part in creating the brand's overall value. The key concept, of course, is that the brand is a shared value because it's built on a base of relationships. While the owner enjoys the profits, the others derive benefits as well. We'll say more about those brand relationships in the next chapter.

3

Separating Hula Hoops
from Viable Brands

Remember Elsie the Cow?

What company did Elsie represent?

What products did she promote?

What was her husband's name?

What were the children's names?

If you answered The Borden Company, dairy products, Elmer, Beulah and Beauregard, you've proven the long-lasting nature of a brand. Or at least you remembered the spokes-cow icon that has lived on in consumer's minds for over seventy years.

"Elsie" was originated in the 1930s as the symbol for The Borden Company, a broad-ranging dairy product company. Appearing initially in a series of print ads, "Elsie" was brought to life on radio in 1938. Expanding the concept, she appeared at the 1939 New York World's Fair. The spokes-cow was so successful that during the 1940s a complete family was created for her. Over the years, Elsie toured fairs, parades, and even helped open Walt Disney World in the 1970s.

In 1997, Elsie and the cow trademarks were licensed to Dairy Farmers of America. Today, Elsie has gone modern with her own web site (www.elsie.com), where she delivers recipes, cooking suggestions, and product information around the world.

So, some brands and their icons, trademarks, and characters have long lives, as has Elsie. And, made lots of profits for the company along the way.

And, in the case of Elsie, value can still be derived from the brand by sale or rights or royalty agreements to another party long after the brand originator has moved on to other businesses.

Now, try this test:

- What company used a sock puppet as its spokesperson?
- On what product did the brand Resistol appear beginning in the 1930s, about the same time Elsie was developed?
- Did you ever own or use an Osborne?
- Did your family gather around the DuMont?

All these terms, titles, and names represented supposedly well-known products, and, the owners thought, brands. The sock puppet was the dot.com darling for Pets.com, the short-lived Internet on-line pet supplies retailer. Resistol was one of the leading men's hat brands until the 1960s, when John Kennnedy and the Beatles convinced men that hats were passé. Osborne was the first portable computer; weighing only 35 pounds, it could, with considerable effort, be transported. And Allen DuMont, one of the originators of the television set, lent his name to one of the 1950s brands of TV sets.

Brands can be longlasting but they're not impervious to change. But, fads, often masquerading as brands, come and go. Remember Bartles & Jaymes, the folksy guys who made wine coolers, or Zima, the beer-type drink of the 1980s, or Clearly Canadian, the watery favorite of the short-lived flavored water craze? The owners of these concepts spent literally millions building what they thought was a brand, only to learn that what they were riding was not a brand at all, only a faddish product line that soared and then crashed. Lots of money out. Not much money back in, at least over the long term.

A simple point: One of the toughest jobs in branding is to know when the product or service deserves the time and effort needed to build a brand and when the concept is merely a flash-in-the-pan.

Any brand's success rests heavily on the product or service concept you've developed and your business model. Those drive the way the "brand" can be developed and how it can and will succeed. And, it has a lot to do with whether you make a lot of money or lose your shirt.

Brands Live On; Fads Flash, Fade, and Die

The beauty of a brand is that it has lasting power. That is, it generally builds and grows year after year. Continuing income flows are what brands are all about.

For example, in the mid-1950s, Philip Morris, the brand owner, and Leo Burnett, their advertising agency, began to convert Marlboro from a woman's cigarette, with a "Mild as May" taste and a lipstick-imprinted filter-tip, to one targeted to men. The initial rebranding campaign featured a tattoo on a man's hand, implying a lean, rugged, outdoorsman—maybe a rancher, or navy officer, or a open-cockpit pilot. The image eventually segued into the western-oriented "Marlboro Man." Now, nearly 50 years later, the "Cowboy" rides around the world, symbolizing and selling the largest and most popular cigarette brand in the world.

So, how does a marketing company develop an "Elsie" or "Marlboro Man" or a "Betty Crocker" or a "Tony the Tiger" or even an "Energizer Bunny"?

Is it skill, planning, or just dumb luck? Or maybe a combination of all three?

Brands Are Learned Skills

Brands survive because customers buy into them. Simply put, that means they live in the hearts and minds of customers. They are part of those people's life experiences. They aren't easily displaced or replaced. They are long-term, high-value products and services for the people who have internalized them. And, they're long-term profit-makers for the brand owners.

However, being able to separate fads and fashions from brands and icons that will live on for years isn't a creative talent. It's a management skill that can be taught and learned. And, that's what the rest of this chapter is all about: separating the wheat from the chaff, the brand "black holes" from the brand bonanzas.

Interestingly, it's not the manager's ability to identify a product or service or facility or country or idea as something that has brand value potential. Instead, it's the ability to identify fads and fashions for what they are: short-term concepts that can be hugely profitable, even though with a limited life span. So, even though you can make a ton of money on a fad—witness the hula hoop, the Cabbage Patch kids and dozens more—we assume you're in the brand business for the long-term returns, not the quick hit, get-in-and-get-out tee-shirt-and-funny-hat fad business. So, if you can tell the difference between a fad and a brand, you're on the way to branding success.

Big-Time Buzz, Small-Time Returns

The problem with fads is they receive huge amounts of immediate attention. They look like can't-miss marketing concepts with unlimited futures. Look at Pets.com. The problem wasn't the brand; it was the business concept. How could anyone, except in the heat of the dot.com mania, believe a company could sell pet food products on-line and then deliver products while relying on the historically miniscule retail pet food margins? You can't spend a dollar and get back ten cents and last very long unless you have extremely deep pockets.

Alternatively, look at what would appear to be a similarly dumb idea: Chia Pets. How could anyone believe a grass-growing, ram-shaped, plant-filled pot, originally promoted on late-night television, turn into a brand. Yet, Chia Pet lives and has for more than 25 years. And, has made a ton of money for its brand owners over the years.

Brands, not fads, create ongoing success.

So, if you want to succeed in branding, look first at your underlying business model. If it's sound, branding is possible. If not, save your dough.

That's also another way to identify a brand babbler. If the babbler starts with obtuse diagrams or geometric shapes or pictures or media plans, get away quick. If the discussion starts with the business model, listen at least for a while before you decide.

One of the biggest babbles in recent times involved Zima, the "not-quite-beer" concept on which Coors spent millions in advertising. The babble revolved around telling people Zima was not a beer.

David Metzger

The Fallacy of "Sure-Fire" Branding Schemes

But, the brand babblers could never quite tell people what it *was*, why they *should* drink it, or what the value proposition was. Lots of money spent. Lots of promotions run. But a bad value proposition. Who wants to buy a "maybe, maybe not beer beverage?"

To sort through the maze, ask yourself: What's the value proposition here? Can this product or service be differentiated from competitors in a meaningful way? And, if it is, then take the next step. Is this something that people will want more than one of, and will they want more than one over time. Brands have ongoing purchasers. Fads have flitting buyers who fly away.

If your analysis says *no* differentiating value proposition, *no* long-term use or requirements, chances are, *no* brand will result no matter how much you spend, how many creative awards you win, or how many people laugh at the jokes. Brands are serious businesses, at least if they involve your money. Treat them that way.

Next stop. Why did Evian and Perrier generate long-term returns for their owners while Clearly Canadian shot up fast, only to splash to earth? Gimmicks. Evian and Perrier had taste, goodness, purity, and health. Clearly Canadian had only a gimmick, flavors. How could anyone buy into the Clearly Candian concept, particularly over the long term? Everyone knows water isn't supposed to taste. In fact, taste in water is almost the antithesis of what water is supposed to be.

So, another way to separate brand babble from business success is to remember: A successful brand can't run counter to common sense. And, common sense is what most brand babblers are lacking.

Many of the brand babblers get caught up in the excitement of new, unique, different, unusual, or one-of-a-kind things. Only problem: Brands are built on a solid base, a value proposition that people can buy into, believe in, respond to, and value year after year. That's the quickest and easiest way to separate the babble of a brand and the base of a brand.

In short, the key ingredients in branding are:

1. Make sure your "to be branded" product or service is based on a solid business model and a sound business proposition.
2. Confirm that that your product or service differentiates itself from competitors with a meaningful value proposition. Slogans and jingles are fine, but, they generally won't pay the rent.
3. Make sure the brand delivers what is truly important to customers and doesn't run counter to common sense.

If your product, service, idea, concept, facility, country, or event doesn't perform on at least two of these three platforms, you likely can't build a sustainable brand no matter how much advertising or promotion or pr or hype or "buzz" you put behind it.

Don't believe us? Try giving your kid a Cabbage Patch doll or a Tickle-Me-Elmo. Or offer one of your friends a Zima (if you can still find one).

How Long Does It Take to Build a Brand?

Brands generally are built over time. That's why you need to think of them as investments. (And, that's another clue about brand babble.

If the babbler suggests your brand will be an instaneous success, button your wallet pocket).

It's true, sometimes brands can be built almost instantaneously, e.g., Starbucks Coffee and Dell Computers and Virgin Airlines and the Blackberry PDA (personal digital assistant). Well, maybe not instantaneously but pretty darn fast.

The key ingredient to understanding how fast your brand will develop generally rests on some type of mass acceptance. One of the top-selling books in the early 2000s was Malcolm Gladwell's *Tipping Points*. Gladwell suggested that public sentiment, conversation, publicity, and being seen in the right places with the right people, could create a mass market reaction for either a new product or the revitalization of an old one.

One of Gladwell's prime examples was the revitalization of Hush Puppies, the soft suede leather leisure shoe first introduced in 1958. Despite its decades of success, by the 1990s, the Hush Puppies brand was so out-of-favor with consumers that it almost disappeared from the marketplace. The brand was literally at death's door until a group of retro young people on Manhattan's Lower East Side suddenly rediscovered Hush Puppies. They thought they were "neat" and "cool," that wearing them as a symbol of their counter-culture, i.e., making a "fashion statement." New York designers saw this new acceptance of Hush Puppies and started to feature them as a hot, trendy fashion item. The revitalized product suddenly became popular again after a twenty-year hiatus.

Why and how did Hush Puppies rise from the dead or dying? Gladwell argues it was because the mysterious "tipping point" was reached. Enough "buzz," promotion and "being in the right places" brought the brand back to life. Suddenly Hush Puppies were "voguish" and riding a wave of popularity. Nothing the brand owner did. It was something that "they" did.

Gladwell can't explain the revitalization of Hush Puppies. We would argue, however, it was the strong and powerful brand Hush Puppies had previously built that enabled the resurrection to occur. The brand was simply latent in the marketplace.

Clearly, the rebirth of Hush Puppies didn't occur because the product was changed or improved or started advertising again. And, it didn't happen because the brand babblers created a new branding diagram or figured out the "brand image" of Hush

Puppies was like a leopard or a gazelle. The business model of Hush Puppies was the same. The value proposition was the same; e.g., wearing Hush Puppies didn't require some change in common sense. It was simply a new twist on an old product. Sometimes, it simply takes a change in consumer consciousness for a brand to be reborn. That seems to be the case with Hush Puppies.

But, there's another key point: Hush Puppies could never have blossomed again if it didn't have some inherent brand value. Suede shoes didn't create the "tipping point" that Gladwell writes about. Nor was it the retro-fashion statement being made by a limited number of designers. It was the brand, Hush Puppies, that made the difference.

So, brands can be resurrected, even when they have suffered years of decline and neglect. Burburry's, Jaguar, and Vanity Fair—along with Hush Puppies—are all testament to a brand's ability to draw on its enduring, inherent qualities to reconnect with groups of customers. Bet the brand babblers are kicking themselves over this one that they didn't see or couldn't call in advance.

How to Build a Brand

Generally, branding gurus, experts, consultants, and the like still believe advertising is the key to building a brand. Invest enough money over a long enough period of time and a brand will occur. And that will happen whether or not it has a sound business model or a solid value proposition or even if it doesn't make common sense. That seems to be industry wisdom, certainly among the brand babblers.

Yet, who remembers the millions spent on the 1999 and 2000 Super Bowls by non-brand-building marketers? In 1999 computer.com spent $2.7 million for two pre-game television commercials plus one spot in the fourth quarter. OurBeginning.com, an online stationery superstore, spent more than $4 million to produce and run a commercial in the SuperBowl broadcast, more than four times its revenue for the first nine months of 1999. That's what the babblers call "making a commitment to the brand." We think it's more like making a commitment to the poor house.

Granted, some of their fellow Super Bowl advertisers, who invested heavily in advertising and promotion during these heady years continue to exist, such as monster.com and E-trade, not to mention "old economy" brands like Budweiser and Nuveen Investments. But, the point is that there are no guarantees in the branding business, and even mega-advertising doesn't always work in building a brand.

"Freebie" Branding

Current industry buzz is that brands can be built with public relations. Some pundits suggest launching a new product and creating a new brand can be done with PR *alone*. Advertising comes along later as support for the established brand. Obviously the advertising people, some of whom are the biggest brand babblers of all, don't like this idea. It suggests advertising isn't very productive or effective in helping establish a new brand or revitalize an old one.

So, a new batch of brand babble has emerged. Advertising or PR? The answer: Yes and no and perhaps (likely) neither, unless the product or service meets the three criteria of the brand platform mentioned above.

Then, there are the big time babblers, the viral marketers— brand babblers who say posting notes on electronic bulletin boards and starting conversations in chat rooms are the best ways to build a brand. Get enough people posting enough notes about your product or service and suddenly, like Gladwell's "tipping point," you have a brand. Sounds good. Sounds cheap. But . . .

The truth is that brands can be built through any of these ways or through none of them. Marketers keep looking for the "silver-bullet" marketing technique that guarantees instant success in brand building. And, that's what most brand babble is about: a silver bullet. A can't-fail approach. A methodology that worked for X number of companies that can work for you. A simple, easy-to-apply brand-building approach that simply can't fail.

But, brands aren't built with tools and techniques and slogans and sayings and posters and light-up buttons. Brands are built through the development of value propositions that are exchanged between between buyers and sellers, between people and organizations, between maker companies and buyer companies.

Brands generally are established, grow, and prosper because they

Exhibit 3.1

BRAND RECIPROCITY MATRIX

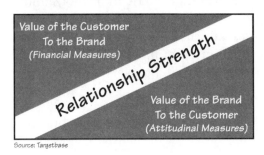

Source: Targetbase

offer some type of reciprocal value between the two or more parties involved in the brand. The brand buyer gets value. The brand seller gets income and profits. This is a reciprocal equation with both sides profiting from the experience—a reciprocal relationship.

Simply put, for a brand to succeed, the marketer must provide value to its customers. And, the customers must provide value to the marketer. So, brands are shared values. Both sides get something out of the relationship.

We don't have many matrices in this book for a reason. Most of them simply complicate what are generally pretty simple ideas. The one in Exhibit 3.1 is no exception. It's called the brand reciprocity matrix. And, as much as we hate these kinds of brand consultant tools, this one illustrates our point.

Above, the vertical line represents the financial value of the customer to the brand. That comes from how customers buy, behave, provide income flows and ultimately profit to the brand owner. The other axis, the vertical one, shows the value the customer gets from the brand. That can be value received, good feelings, beliefs about use or the like. In short, they are the perceptions, beliefs, and feelings about the brand that provide value and assurance and make the brand desirable and valuable for the customer.

When the "brand value to the customer" and the "customer value to the brand" are balanced, the brand will grow and succeed over time. But, there must be reciprocal balance. Both sides must benefit. Without mutual benefit, no product, service, element, concept, or anything else can gain the title of "brand."

This shared value, the cooperative nature of the brand is one of the key elements of brands and branding that is too often over-looked by the so-called "brand-builders." Branding is building re-ciprocal value, not just an exercise in navel-gazing.

With this view of how to differentiate a brand from a hula hoop, we move to a discussion of brand-building research—an area where you can drop a ton of money in a hurry and not know any more than when you started. Babblers are prevalent. So beware.

4

Dogs, Pigeons, Focus Groups and Other Exotic Brand Research Techniques

if people would only behave like they are supposed to or in ways that fit the brand babblers' models, branding would be a piece of cake. But they don't. And it isn't. And, as a result, brand research is expensive, takes a lot of time, and often provides limited benefits.

It would seem natural: Learning more about what people think and want and do—i.e., research—would provide useful answers.

But, unfortunately, research is not and has not always been the friend of the brand owner. Research babble is generally the most complex, difficult to understand, and confusing of all the brand discussions. Much of that comes from the opposing views of whether attitudes or behaviors provide the best explanation of how consumers deal with brands. Researchers get tangled up in debate, and the brand owner gets tangled up in costly and often conflicting studies. Thus, research has hurt brand understanding almost as much as it has helped.

Remember Chapter 2 and all the babble about who owns the

brand? Research created some of this babble, and other babble as well. The only difference here: The babble has been piled higher and broader.

Blame It on Freud (and Maybe His Mother)

The biggest brand marketing problem researchers have created are the underlying psychological models they have developed. Models you, as the brand owner, pay for, but from which you may get little return.

The equation the research folks have developed is easy to understand. Marketing and brands deal with people. So, if people buy products and services, and if we understand them (e.g., their hidden motives, psyches, drives, motivations, and the like), we can find better or more effective ways to sell them things or services or ideas. Sounds easy enough, doesn't it?

So, people are the reason marketing researchers latched onto psychological models and applied or misapplied them to marketing.

Beginning in the middle part of the twentieth century, advertising and marketing people accepted and adapted the work of Freud, Pavlov, Skinner, and a host of other psychology mavens as the basis for the discipline: people and how they think. That's why there is so much psychological mumbo-jumbo underlying the ways marketing, advertising, and promotion people talk about how they plan, develop, implement, and even measure the impact of advertising, promotion, and branding.

Girding most "advertising" models (we'll use the term *advertising* here to cover the entire gamut of marketing communication theory) are two research streams. One is the work of Pavlov, who demonstrated dogs could be trained to react to certain continuously reinforced stimuli and Skinner, who demonstrated that repetition had a big impact on pigeons. In short, if the same stimuli were used often enough, dogs and pigeons would learn and respond to various cues. Surely, the same thing would work with people. That's where much of our "advertising theory" comes from: People learn like dogs and pigeons.

Of course, the researchers threw in some of Freud's work to get to "underlying motives," the personal psyche, hopes and dreams, and the like.

Those are the underpinnings of modern day advertising, marketing, and branding: Stimulus response models with a bit of inner-self and sex thrown in for good measure.

Building a Castle on a Flimsy Base

This is how advertising research developed as well. Psychological models of how consumers remember, think, act, believe, respond, and so on. Borrow a bit from here, tag on a bit from there, and, at some point, you have a "people-based advertising model." That's the basic idea advertising and branding research managers have been "developing" and "improving" and "enhancing" for the past hundred years.

The only problem is: The model may well be wrong. Thus, many, if not most, of our research techniques may be wrong as well.

But, because we have such a wide and deep base of literature, experiments, models, and folklore based on the historical models, marketers and other brand babblers are loath to consider anything different. It's easier to go with the flow than to try to change things. And it's a whole lot more profitable for the researchers as well.

A Logical Disconnect
(or an Illogical Connect) in 1961

One would think, advertising has always been about sales. That started back when man first began to draw crude pictures. If you advertised, sales were supposed to go up. If you didn't advertise, nobody knew you or trusted your product. Sales didn't grow. Your company went bankrupt and your children went without shoes. That was the common understanding about advertising up until 1961. Then it changed.

Having digested the psychological work on how people were supposed to behave, advertising people determined a more sophisticated approach was needed. True, there were reasons. Multilevel distribution channels were developing. Mass media was emerging. Consumers were moving toward discretionary spending. In short, the old "cause and effect" model of advertising was increasingly harder to develop and considerably harder to prove.

In 1961 two "advertising" models emerged. They have driven

Exhibit 4.1

TRADITIONAL "HIERARCHY OF EFFECTS" VIEW OF COMMUNICATION

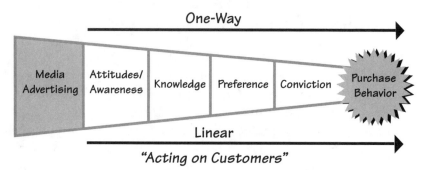

advertising thinking ever since, and they have had a major influence on brands and branding as well. One, called the "Hierarchy of Effects," was a hypothetical model of how "advertising" was supposed to work. Developed by Lavidge and Steiner,[1] it underlies all advertising today. The other, by consultant Russell Colley, suggested essentially the same model.[2] He developed it for the Association of National Advertisers and called it DAGMAR (Designing Advertising Goals for Measured Advertising Response).

Both of these models assumed some type of identifiable attitudinal change occurred among people as they moved or were moved toward the purchase of a product or service. Thus, the hypothesis was that people followed a certain path in deciding what they needed or wanted and how they might identify the product or service that would fill their needs.

The Hierarchy of Effects and DAGMAR models both assumed that if the advertiser knew these consumer paths, he or she could influence the direction and speed of consumer movement and, therefore, consumer purchases. Therefore, with the right advertising investment at the right time, marketers could "manipulate" consumers and influence their purchases. See the connection now between dogs and pigeons and people?

The Hierarchy of Effects model is illustrated in Exhibit 4.1. The DAGMAR model is an almost mirror image.

The Hierarchy is clearly a linear model. Consumers are always moving forward toward some purchase behavior. The advertiser, in effect, pushes them through the process with advertising. Thus, the

David Metzger

"But how do you <u>really</u> <u>feel</u> about your brand?"

more advertising toward customers or prospects, the faster they move toward purchase, and the more likely it is the purchase decision will favor the advertiser.

The Hierarchy's appeal is that the marketer controls the system. The more money the advertiser puts against the people through advertising, the faster they move through the process and the faster they purchase the product or service. That's the premise, although the model has never been proven in the marketplace.

What marketers like is that the people can't get off or change or regress once the advertiser starts communicating with them. It assumes that people are like the Pavlovian dogs and the Skinnerian pigeons, being trained to perform as the advertiser wants them to perform. Marketers like this idea. It gives them control over seemingly uncontrollable customers.

Ignoring a Critical Step

Strangely enough, although the Hierarchy and DAGMAR look like performance-based models, they aren't. Using this model, researchers in 1961 successfully disconnected advertising from sales. They argued advertising should be judged on attitudinal change, not sales. In other words, while the model goal was "Purchase Behavior," advertising measures always stopped short of that influential step.

Most advertising managers argue, therefore, they can only be responsible for "communication effects," i.e., movement along the attitudinal chain up to the point of actual behavior. The rationale they offered for this "advertising interruptus," is that too many "intervening variables" occur to take on sales responsibility. Too many product stocking problems, competitive marketplace offers, misaligned pricing, and a multitude of other things not under their control. That prevents them from "closing the loop" on sales. Thus, advertising managers take credit for "communication movement" along the Hierarchy but have avoided any responsibility for sales.

Basically, advertising researchers were right in the 1960s. At that time, the marketplace had become too complex for the simple Pavlovian and Skinnerian cause-and-effect models. Marketing organizations simply couldn't tie general market advertising directly to sales. Of course, there were exceptions, such as direct marketing or sales promotion, but those were considered "below-the-line" and beneath the scrutiny of advertising people.

There were, however, other reasons why the Hierarchy model didn't work. We save these for Chapter 5.

How Everyone Learned to Love the Hierarchy Model

Every marketing communication executive loved the Hierarchy model. Advertising managers, because they were now responsible only for "communication effects," not sales. Academicians because they could now bring in sociology, diffusion theory, anthropology, and other esoteric approaches. Researchers because they could fool around with measures of awareness, preference, and recall using statistical tools few lay people understood. Everybody got something from the Hierarchy model except the brand owner. He or she spent money and got recall, intent, liking, and a host of other "effects" but no connection to sales and profits.

Remember: Brands are supposed to create sales and profits, but not just for the researcher. *For the brand owner!*

Agencies and the media loved the Hierarchy of Effects model, too, because it was essentially a "tonnage" model. It assumed that the more money the advertiser spent, i.e., buying space or time or messages, the greater or faster the movement along the Hierarchy scale. Thus, the advertiser was encouraged to increase spending to improve results: A neat equation, for the agencies focused on media commissions, and the media focused on frequency purchases of advertising.

Again, lots of sales and profits for the agency and the media. Questionable returns for the brand owner.

And, everyone else loved the Hierarchy of Effects model because it solved one of the most basic advertising problems: How to measure some kind of effect without becoming committed to sales. With the Hierarchy, advertisers and marketers could move to various forms of statistical analysis and modeling based on questionnaires, population sampling and marketplace projections. Small numbers of people could be asked relatively simple questions and heroic assumptions could be made about the potential impact and results of the advertising program. What a great, statistically supportable, graph and chart-filled addition to presentations the Hierarchy made! And, what a neat bundle of expensive and easy-to-conduct research packages for the advertising and marketing research community!

Again, money for the researchers. Undefinable returns for the brand owner.

That's where we are today: Advertising research techniques based on models of awareness, recall, and supposed preference, and measurement of movement along a hypothetical scale. But, only to an end point that keeps moving farther off into the horizon as you begin to approach it. Research based on samples and projections using attitudinal questionnaires among the relevant populations. It's a neat package for measuring communication effects and ignoring sales. And selling research studies.

The only problem? There is not, and never has been, any valid proof that the Hierarchy of Effects exists or can be measured. It has never been more than an unproven hypothesis even though it is elegantly intuitive and justifiably rational. Sadly, for the past fifty years, researchers have been unable to verify the Hierarchy. William Weilbacher, writing in the *Journal of Advertising Research* in 2001 said: "Hierarchy models of advertising effects are little more than rationally and intuitively sensible."[3]

The Trap Is Set and Branders Fall Right In

The biggest problem for branding is that these professionals, consultants, academicians, researchers and gurus, i.e., all those who have been involved "professing" on how brands are developed and babbling about how brands are built and managed, have bought into this advertising-based attitudinal model. That's why most brand research has to do with attitudinal models based on psychological questions drawn from relatively small numbers of people that are then projected to the whole. The assumption, of course, is that there are large number of "average people" who fit a normally distributed statistical curve.

Just look at today's brand research approaches: focus groups, indepth interviews, psychological projections, trade-off analysis and the like. You won't find much large-scale brand research. And, what does exist uses attitudinal change as the primary value to be gained. Again, the assumption that attitudinal change will lead to behavioral change. More dog and pigeon concepts applied to people. Shades of the 1960s all over again.

The use of advertising-originated attitudinal models also explains much of the research done to track the effects of brand communication. Many of those models borrowed from psychology as well. The most common brand-tracking research approaches are those loosely based on a model developed by A. H. Maslow in the 1940s.[4] Maslow suggested that human motivations can be categorized in a hierarchy. He based them on five levels of need beginning at the base with physiological needs, i.e., food, shelter, clothing, etc., followed by the need for safety, for belongingness and love, for esteem, and finally, at the highest level, for self-actualization. (Sounds a bit like the Hierarchy of Effects model, doesn't it?) It also explains why brand and branding research gurus ask such interesting questions as "How do you feel about Brand X as compared to Brand Y in terms of helping you meet a need for cleanliness? Or a need to moisturize your skin? Or a need/desire to feel beautiful?" The objective, of course, is to understand what motivates buyers and users, and to understand the conscious and subconscious associations they might make with a brand and its usage.

Done well, such research gives brand managers valuable insights into the feelings, emotions, and attitudes about one brand compared to another. Done improperly (as is often the case), such research can drain a big hole in a budget while leading the research to either meaningless or, worse, totally incorrect conclusions.

Clearly, today, the connection between brand research and brand returns leads through the groves of psychology. But, there are a number of detours, routes under construction, dead-ends and cul-de-sacs. So, there's money in research for the researchers, but a much less direct connection to returns for the brand owner.

If you look at the kinds of research being used today to understand brands, much of it is psychological in nature and most of it has been borrowed from the advertising people. Perhaps some of the approaches and techniques should be returned as defective.

Static Models, Dynamic People

The problem, however, is not that qualitative research is inherently bad. The problem is: Much brand research is badly conceived and based on incorrect assumptions.

Generally, marketing research is focused on projecting what might happen if attitude change did occur; e.g., what people might do, given their knowledge, background, hopes, and dreams based on their feelings and attitudes about the brand. They assume people tomorrow will be an extension of people today—or that how people feel today will likely be how they will feel tomorrow. And that people really know and can express why they do the things they do, particularly about products and services ranging from breakfast cereal to automobiles to pest controllers.

Unfortunately, people are notoriously inaccurate in explaining their own feelings and motivations or in predicting their future actions. Few can really accurately say what they will do tomorrow or the next week. And asking people to predict what they might buy further into the future, say three to five years out, is even more speculative. The basic problem is: The models are static and people and the marketplace are dynamic. Thus, getting accurate predictions about future purchases or uses or even attitudes is not just incredibly difficult, it's often wrong. People don't really know what they will do in the future. Asking them a number of hypothetical questions certainly doesn't improve their predictive qualifications one whit.

So, in short, brands suffer from the same research challenges that have plagued, and often baffled, advertising researchers for more than a century.

But, the problem is more complex today.

Behavioral Data Challenges the Existing Research Models

One reason advertising managers wanted to move away from behavioral and financial measures of advertising was simple. Until, fairly recently, it was extremely difficult, if not impossible, to gather and manage the actual transactional data that could link communication activities to sales.

So, marketing and communication researchers did the best they could with the tools they had. They built hypothetical, attitudinally-based models . . . i.e., the Hierarchy of Effects. They sampled consumers and prospects. They asked questions trying to capture data they could code, aggregate, and analyze. Because, in the middle 1960s, they couldn't possibly handle all the behavioral data records, they sampled the population. Then they used statistical techniques to project those small samples to the total population. Thus, they had explanations and predictions and hypotheses and solutions that were certainly better than personal estimations by the sales force or senior management—but, often, not by much.

Technology changed the system. Today, behavioral data is flooding the market. Many marketing organizations are awash in what customers actually did or have done in the marketplace. Point-of-sale purchases, frequent shopper and loyalty programs, trackable coupons, cookies attached to Internet sites and the like flood the researchers' desktops. All identify and connect specific customers to specific marketplace behaviors and, most of all, to specific products or services. So, the question today is not "What did customers do?" The better question is: "Why did they do it?" for we commonly know who the customers are, what they have bought from us over time, what prices they paid, to what promotions they responded and a host of other things. But, often we *still* don't know why. And current attitudinal models, commonly based on projections of future intentions, don't help. We're stuck with a 1960s model in a twenty-first century marketplace.

This growing availability of behavioral data has created the current schism in the marketing, advertising, and branding world. That is, should the advertiser or marketer commit to an attitudinal or behavioral model of customer explanation and projection? If I use attitudinal data, I will know how people feel about my brand and what I might do to get them to change their feelings. But, I can't project those feelings into actual behaviors that result in sales because the data is based on models that are not connected to sales.

Alternatively, if I commit to behavioral data, I know what people did or have done but, I know little or understand less why they did it.

Thus, it is this dichotomy within the marketing organization—Should we use attitudinal or behavioral data to build the brand's explanatory, persuasion, and response models?—that's creating today's problems for brand owners.

The answer, of course, is today's marketer likely need both. No, that doesn't mean you double your spend on research. It simply means you have to think differently about your research needs.

The reciprocal model (The Brand Reciprocity Matrix in Chapter 3) is just that: behavioral data of what people have done in the marketplace that can be related to attitudinal data about the importance of the brand to the consumer. When you put the two together, you can start to get some answers.

The problem is that too many organization and their supporting brand consultants, have created artificial barriers between the attitudinal and behavioral data. They seem committed to one or the other but seldom to both. The babblers like to keep this argument going. Behavioral or attitudinal. Silos. Separation. Historical or projective? All play into the hands of the brand mavens. Divide and conquer. Combine and risk the growth of knowledge.

Much of today's babble is bound up in this question of attitudinal or behavioral data. That's what has created many of the issues in brand measurement. Traditionally, brand researchers have tended to concentrate on such tracking mechanisms as brand recall, recognition, and supposed preference. Alternatively, the focus of the database analysts has been on analyzing purchase patterns among highly specific customer segments. What is really needed is a greater integration of all customer insights and behavioral data. That will give a much truer picture of the customer's value to the brand and the value of the brand to the customer.

What should the brand owner do?

First, understand the "attitudinal and behavioral babble."

Recognize the basis on which the researchers are developing their proposals. They can't connect attitudinal data to future purchases so don't get caught up in the Hierarchy of Effects. Second, if you can get behavioral data, use it first. It at least shows what people have done in the past. It is a direct connection between people and sales. Putting your money on known behaviors is better than betting on lots of conjecture.

Remember. You can spend lots of money on research. And, you can generate lots of profits for the researchers. The key, however, is how can you make a profit on your brand. If you can't directly connect the proposed research to direct increases in your brand's sales, take another look. There are lots of alternatives. The key question is: Which one is right for you?

Notes

1. Robert J. Lavidge and Gary A. Steiner, "A Model for Predictive Measurements Advertising Effectiveness," *Journal of Marketing*, October 1961.
2. Russell H. Colley, *Defining Advertising Goals for Measured Advertising Results*, New York, Association of National Advertisers, 1961
3. William Weilbacher, "Does Advertising Cause A 'Hierarchy of Effects'?" *Journal of Advertising Research*, November/December 2001.
4. A. H. Maslow, "A Theory of Human Motivation" *Psychology Review*, 50:370–396, 1943.

5

Mental Models, S-Curves and Multi-Tasking

Chapter Four illustrated why much of today's brand babble is focused on attitudinal change. The babbling occurs because the proposed models are supposed to measure financial impact and effect of brand investments—but they don't. We'll deal with how to really measure brand returns in later chapters. For the moment, we need to persuade you that advertising models and approaches have a limited amount of impact on building or maintaining a brand.

Because advertising was used to build brands fifty years ago doesn't mean it's the most efficient or effective way to build them today. Unfortunately, in this case, experience isn't the best teacher in brand building. Building brands in the twenty-first century is nothing like building them in the twentieth century was. And, that's important to know when wading through the brand babble.

The Tailspin and Death Spiral of the P&G Branding Model

Probably no organization was better at building brands in the twentieth century than P&G. Taking what were essentially commodity products, differentiating them slightly and then hammering home "dream-building" brand messages through massive repetition with "slice-of-life" television commercials, helped generate huge sales and created incredibly powerful brands. And, made P&G tons of money along the way. Most marketers can cite chapter and verse on the P&G successes simply because they're now household words . . . Tide, Cheer, Charmin, Jif, Pringles, Bounce, Crest, and on and on.

P&G managers knew how to build brands and they maximized that knowledge to the nth degree. It was formulaic, predictable, based on massive advertising investments. And it worked. P&G advertised. People bought.

But, as important, most other package goods manufacturers learned the same lessons, or maybe they learned from P&G, i.e., Unilever, Kraft, Colgate-Palmolive, Gillette, Nestle, Mars, and others. Same model. Same approach. And, in most cases, success after success. Big advertising investments. Big returns. Big profits.

The problem that developed was that everyone believed the P&G model was "the" brand-building model and that it was replicable. And it was. But only for consumer package goods products and only during the 1950s to 1970s. Unfortunately, the babblers only got half the story. That's why today the model often fails more than it succeeds.

The reason P&G and the other fmcgs were successful with their "brand-building" model was that they controlled the entire marketing and branding system from start to finish. We discussed this idea of marketer control in Chapter 2. If you have control of your marketplace, you might be able to replicate the model. But, if you don't, don't believe the babble that goes with the package goods approach to branding.

The moral of the story: P&G built brands. Huge brands. Massive brands. Great financial resources for the company. And all based on a nonreplicable model.

We say nonreplicable for a reason. P&G built their model and succeeded during a time when all the stars were aligned just right. A post-World War II population boom. Incredible developments in technology. Radically changing distribution systems. Increasing consumer disposable income. Big changes in consumer transportation. But, most of all, the development of audience-aggregating mass communication systems featuring the addictive communication narcotic called television—something the world had never seen before.

The problem is: We'll never see that star alignment again in the developed economies. Yes, you can find this system emerging after a fashion in economies such as China, India, and Eastern Europe, but don't try to make it work in France or Japan or Australia. Those markets are way beyond the "advertise and grow" model that worked in the US thirty to forty years ago.

Psychologically-Challenged Models

Thinking back, it's easy to see how the P&G model of brand building, built on psychological concepts introduced by Pavlov, Skinner, Maslow, and others, worked. Consumers were trained to buy P&G products much like Skinner trained his pigeons to respond to food. Repetition and reward. Show them a demonstration commercial over and over again on television or repeat the same message continuously on "soap opera" radio. Promise them a reward of "cleaner" or "whiter" or "brighter" and American consumers were ready and happy to buy and re-buy.

The wrinkle? Today, we know the "stimulus-response" model of Pavlov and the others is not really how the human mind works, at least not when there are alternatives and variables. Controlled experiments in restricted surroundings is not the arena in which today's customers operate. Thus, most of the "behaviorist" concepts of Skinner, Pavlov, and others, which provide the base for advertising theorists and brand babblers, are being seriously challenged.

The reason: Behaviorist models are passé. If they ever described the world accurately, it's a world that no longer exists. Cognitive models better describe how the brain, the mind, and the people "work." They are the basis of most current psychology. The problem is: Advertising models are hung up on stimulus-response theory and just can't shake the old concepts.

Cognitive psychology suggests the human mind is a vast interactive network of nodes and nodules, bits and pieces, concepts and content that are influenced by electrical impulses and chemical changes. Thus, memory "works" by allowing the mind to piece together numerous bits and bites of information, data, experiences, and the like—all assembled for a specific purpose and all on demand. So, brands are not stored away in a "slot" or in a "cranial niche" like the positioning gurus say. Instead, they are instantly assembled, on demand, to meet certain needs and requirements. Brands are continuously changing, being revised, revamped, reviewed, and the bits and pieces retained for future assembling as needed. In short, the human mind and memory is a continuous "work-in-progress."

Brands are scraps and experiences that every person assembles for him or herself. (See Chapter 2.) That's why, even though the individual consumer assembles the brand him or herself, the inputs and impact of that brand come from the experiences the consumer has with the people who make up the brand just as much as they do with the product or service. In short, the brand comes from what it delivers on a regular basis, not on what it promises. Brand promises are nice for brand marketers, but brand experiences are what drive continuing sales.

Questions Raised but Not Answered

This new view of how the mind works raises some interesting questions about brands. If every person assembles the brand for him or herself, what does that do to the concept of "brand positioning"?

Positioning assumes every person, everywhere, every time will view the brand in exactly the same way. That every brain will assemble all the same bits and pieces in the same order and come up with the same solution or same image every time.

Not likely.

So, given what we know today, Coca-Cola may have several billion brand images or brand positions, depending on how many people know or have had experience with the brand. And, while Coke will and must strive for some type of brand consistency, this new view of "brain operation" explains why Coca-Cola can have advertising featuring polar bears, groups of children singing on a hillside in Italy and hard-core rock'n'roll music, all at the same time and all successfully communicating what Coca-Cola is and what it is all about. So, save your money on the big positioning studies. They cost a lot and you learn only a little.

Because of our new understanding of cognitive psychology, the image of Coca-Cola depends to a large extent on the person assembling and experiencing the image, not just on what Coca-Cola says in its advertising and brand communication.

We're not saying you can send your brands off willy-nilly in any creative direction the wild-eyed art director says. Discipline and good judgment are still necessary. However, what it does say is that brands don't likely follow the traditional model in spite of what the advertising-oriented branding consultants and gurus say. More babble. Less relevance. More money in their pockets for these historical models. Less money in your pocket when they don't work.

So, remember: Brands are not necessarily advertising-driven. True, advertising can help. But, simply spending a lot of money on a brand advertising campaign doesn't guarantee success, and it certainly doesn't guarantee you will even get your investment back. The dot.coms proved that in the late 1990s. You don't need to learn that lesson for yourself.

So, how do people learn about products and services that would like to turn themselves into brands? That's next.

When Did the S-Curve Die?

Part of the problem of hanging brand and branding development on advertising theory is that much of that is either wrong or irrelevant in today's marketplace. Take the Sigmoid or S-Curve for example.

For over half a century, advertising planning has been based on the premise of a Sigmoid or "S-curve." This is the famous "learning curve" that comes straight out of Pavlov and Skinner. It's based on simple repetition; i.e., if you repeat an advertising message enough, people will learn it. (The concept is illustrated as Part A of Exhibit 5.1.)

The problem with the S-curve is that people may learn your message but do nothing about it. For example, think of the great number of people who can hum the Chevrolet "Like a Rock" jingle but have never bought or may never buy a Chevrolet pickup. Learning and doing are two different things.

Clearly, it's media by the pound with the S-curve. Or, maybe it's media by the ton. Maybe that's why advertising agencies and the media like the S-curve. It's based on the use of huge numbers of media exposures and giant advertising budgets. If repetition creates

Exhibit 5.1

MEDIA RESPONSE ASSUMPTIONS

S Curve   Convex Curve

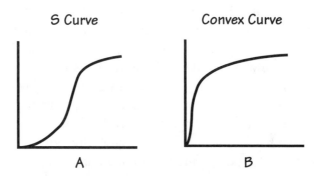

A   B

learning or at least the ability to retain or store information in the brain, then the more, the better.

The babblers will cite chapter and verse on this memory-recall connection. And, most of their examples came from memory experiments, some dating back to the 1890s. True, with enough repetition people can perform certain functions. That's what athletics and practice are all about. Examples are always given about how a person learns to drive a car or learns to swim or how to play soccer. And there is truth in the learning curve. It does work. But, being able to remember an advertising slogan doesn't mean you have any interest in or need for the product. That's where the babblers leave off and your money starts to disappear.

What happened, of course, is that advertising theorists took the S-curve and applied it to media planning. They made the assumption that repetition of an advertising message or commercial could or would result in the exposed audience "learning" about the product or the benefit or the jingle or the slogan or whatever. That's where we got the concepts of reach, (the number of people exposed or who had the opportunity to see or hear the commercial) and frequency (the number of times they were likely to see or hear it, or, better said, had the *opportunity* to see or hear it).

The problem with the S-curve is that it may apply when learning to drive a car, but it may not be so applicable in terms of how people screen, take in, and store advertising materials and messages. So, reach and awareness are fine to the extent that people can't buy something they don't know about. (Although they do seem to collapse that process very quickly, as evidenced by the purchase of impulse products). Unfortunately, it's of little real help if you don't know where the people are or how they are processing your message.

Why Gus Got Gored

Back in the 1980s, the media director at S. C. Johnson & Sons in Racine, Wisconsin, Gus Premier, wrote a book titled *Effective Media Planning* in which he challenged the S-curve in advertising.[1] His research work showed that the then-called "advertising response curve" was not an S at all but a convex curve, such as the one illustrated in Part B of Exhibit 5.1. In other words, advertising did not "build up" over time through repetition. Instead, the greatest impact or the greatest learning from advertising, certainly for consumer products, came from the first exposure the consumer had to it. Once that first exposure occurred (or *opportunity to be seen* happened), while the learning and the value of the advertisement or commercial continued to increase, it did so at a continuously decreasing rate. In other words, people seem to learn all they want or need to know about a product or service on the first exposure. The rest of the exposures end up being reminders.

What Gus did was to challenge the entire advertising community: i.e., the Hierarchy of Effects, the S-Curve, and, along with that, the entire media planning process.

Well, guess what happened to Gus. He was roundly criticized, his work poo-pooed, and his reputation stained forever. No advertising person wanted to have advertising theory challenged, and certainly not those who made their living based on the Hierarchy concept that said "more is better" and "excess is even better still."

So, when the branding revolution began in the mid-1980s, Gus' concept of convex curves was ignored in favor of the more widely accepted S-curves. Branding gurus and consultants and brand managers traipsed off along the "reach and frequency" trail, and that is where most brand development media planning is today.

Your acceptance or rejection of the S-curve or the convex curve has much to do with how you build or maintain a brand. If you buy into the S-curve, you spend huge amounts of money in advertising and other forms of marketing communication trying to drive the message or picture or concept or value of the brand into the minds of customers and prospects. The assumption, of course, is that you will get something back from all that recall, recognition, image playback, and the like. Spend money. Get attitudes and memory and recall back. Not a terribly successful approach in a financially-driven marketplace.

If you accept Gus' convex curve, you may spend the same amount of money, but you spend it quite differently. Rather than having one message, you might have many, all on the same theme, of course. And you likely would present them in a number of ways so that your brand message was always fresh, interesting, and innovative. And you probably would accept the fact that people are getting information and material from lots of sources, not just from your advertising and promotion programs. And, most importantly, you would likely also recognize that information was coming from people involved and associated with the brand. So, you likely would focus on media and message integration and how all those messages would help develop and extend your brand strategy and implementation. In other words, you might have polar bears and kids singing on a hillside and even rock-'n'roll bands promoting your brand—successfully.

It takes guts to move away from the S-curve simply because it has so many supporters. But, there is one basic reason why you should: That's how you will find your customer or help your customer find you.

The Multi-Tasking Consumer

Traditional advertising media planning theories and approaches are all based on one basic assumption: that the person being exposed is focused on that particular medium and that medium alone and thus the message being delivered and that message alone during the time of exposure. So, you are "watching television" or "reading the newspaper" or "listening to the radio." Singular, focused attention. The mind ready and anxious to take in the information or messages the marketer is sending.

The problem: Even if that was the way advertising happened during the last century, it's not what happens today. Today's consumers operate in a multi-textured milieu where they are networked, interactive, and instantly connected to everything around them. They use a multitude of communication systems all at the same

David Metzger

The Multi-tasking Consumer

time. They are multi-tasking individuals who are doing, or at least trying to do, several things at once.

In October, 2002, Don Schultz and Joe Pilotta presented a paper at the US-based Advertising Research Foundation "Week of Workshops" in New York. They reported on research conducted with over 7,500 individuals on their media usage and habits. The findings? Over 50 percent of all the people surveyed reported they were using multiple media during a single point in time. They were reading the newspaper and watching television or they were online and listening to the radio or they were online, watching television and reading a magazine all at the same time. In short, they were multi-tasking with media.

So much for audience measurement.

Since media theory and measurement assume single focus, single attention to a single medium at any one point in time, this simultaneous media usage information throws everything up in the air. And it certainly raises major questions about how the marketing organization can develop brand planning programs using the "tried and true" advertising concepts on which so many of the models are based. For example: How do you define an "unduplicated audience" when you have simultaneous media usage? Or how do you measure "reach" when people are using multiple media at the same time?

Lots of questions. Few answers in today's media planning, buying, or measurement systems. In short, do you want to really put your faith in a system that is known to be flawed and gamble your hard-earned dollars on models that have been proven useless? That's what many of the babblers are asking you to do.

Traditional forms of media are being challenged, and the basic concepts of how brands are built and maintained should be questioned as well. In short, there are real problems in relying on advertising-based concepts to build and maintain brands. But, that is what is happening, often to the detriment of the brand and certainly the organization.

Nevertheless, the question still stands: If traditional advertising is a dead end or even worse, a bottomless pit, where can we go to help build and grow our brands so that we profit from their value?

Hopefully, the next chapter will start to answer some of the questions we have raised.

Notes

1. August Premier, *Effective Media Planning*, Lexington Books, Lexington, MA, 1989.

6

Reification, Abstactionism, Tribal Dances and Other Incantations About Brands and Branding

In a recent article in one of the leading U.S. management magazines, a group of professors suggested a brand might be evaluated using a matrix with four quadrants: The quadrants were "enacted" vs. "functional" and "reified vs. abstract." Whoo boy!

In a brand conference not too long ago, the opening session consisted of a group of African tribal dancers "expressing" themselves and relating to brands and branding. Wow!

And, a review of recently published books on branding uncovered topics as esoteric as the symbolic, linguistic, and semiotic aspects of branding, emotional branding, fusion branding, cult branding, the DNA of brands, and the role of brands as archetypes.

The brand babblers have clearly taken over the asylum.

Brands have come a long way from the old days when the brand was the family name of the maker, (Wedgewood, Kraft, or Kellogg) or the location where the product was made (Waterford Crystal or Chicago Cutlery). Today, brands have been studied, dissected, anthropoligized, socialized, depth-interviewed, and just plain hyperbolized to the point that we are losing sight of the basic function. Brand are things marketing organizations use to try and make more money. Brands are investments for sure. But, they need to pay some returns to the owners. Creating nifty, complex, complicated advertising concepts generally doesn't make any money for anyone other than the babbler.

Simply Put: Brands Are Relationships

In their simplest form, brands are the manifestation (see, we know big words, too) of some type of relationship between the buyer and the seller. True, we attach names and symbols and icons to brands in the marketplace. And, sometimes we even hide the name of the manufacturer or seller to give the brand more "cachet."

But, the fact remains: Brands exist simply because the supplier provides something that customers like and that gives them some value beyond simply another chocolate cookie with a white icing center.

Brands are really quite simple. They are the things that define a relationship between the buyer and the seller. And that relationship can come in many different forms.

For example, in human relationships we have all levels. We have relationships with people we love and people we really dislike. We have strong relationships, such as family, and perhaps somewhat weaker relationships with work colleagues. We have good friends and we have acquaintances. And, we have ongoing and often casual and fleeting relationships.

Brands are no different.

The problem with brands is how the term "relationship" has been and is being used and mis-used. That's where the babbling is getting everyone all tangled up.

So, let's cut through the show-biz, the magic incantations, the narcissistic analogies, and the impenetrable discussions of brand symbolism to get to the core idea of brand relationships.

To start, we take a brief tour of relationships as they have been applied to marketing and now to branding.

Once upon a Time in the Frozen North . . .

Guess where "relationship marketing" and the concept of relationships between buyers and sellers originated. If you said Finland and Sweden, you'd be right.

In the early 1980s, Christian Gronroos at the Hanken School of Business in Helsinki and Evart Gummeson at the University of Stockholm began working on the concepts that underlie today's marketing of services and ultimately customer relationships.

Their premise: Unlike manufactured products, services rely on people to deliver much of their value. And when you bring people into the equation, brands take on all kinds of new meanings. (Recall our discussion in Chapter 2.)

Gronroos and Gummeson argued that in "services marketing" customers relied as much on their relationships with the people involved or those who delivered the brand value at least as much and generally more than they did on the "physical product." So, during the 1980s and into the middle 1990s, Gronroos and Gummeson and their supporters developed the basic ideas behind "relationship marketing." Successfully, we might add.

Everything was going nicely for relationship marketing until the middle 1990s. That's when the technologists "hijacked" the term Customer Relationship Management or CRM. Siebel, Epiphany, and a number of other software developers took what was originally a sales force allocation and contact management software model designed to optimize sales activities and called it CRM. Their promise: "You can 'manage' your customers by gathering, analyzing, and automating your external contacts with them."

Marketers bought into the concept, ignoring the fact that "relationships" come from personal contacts, conversations, dialogs and ongoing experiences, not marketer-initiated and delivered monologues, sell-ups, or sell-ons.

Unfortunately, the concepts involving "brand relationship" have sometimes taken on the meanings the software developers gave them, not the basic understanding of human relationships that Gronroos and Gummeson were advocating. And that's where we are today. So, if you've sunk bags of money into a CRM application and can't figure out why you've gotten more problems than solutions or found the software investments to be the "black hole of cap-ex," now you know why. Software can't match human relationships no matter how many "bells and whistles" are put on the software package.

There's No Relationship in Relationship Marketing

Relationship marketing or management or whatever, at least as it has developed in North America, is not based on any type of relationship. It's based on optimizing external, generally outbound marketing programs where the marketer wants to up-sell, cross-sell, or direct-sell to automatically identified prospects.

So, when you start to talk about "relationships," whether they are "customer relationships," "brand relationships," or even "personal relationships," be careful that you really mean human interactions and interfaces and not ones based on some type of "yield management" designed to "optimize returns" from a group of "target markets."

You can spend a lot going out and never see a lot coming back in.

Intellectual Bonds May Better

A "brand relationship" is some type of bond—financial, physical, or emotional—that brings the brand seller and buyer together. Thus, the relationship can be either deep or shallow. Rational or irrational. Long term or short term. Or any combination in between.

The critical element is the need for reciprocity. Recall our discussion in Chapter 3. There must be benefit to both the buyer and the seller. And that has generally been the problem with the so-called "relationship marketing" programs that have been foisted off on corporate clients for the past decade . . . lots of value for the software developer but little value for the marketer, and even less for the customer

Relationships are not computer-generated, no matter how sophisticated the software or how exotic the customer classification schemes. More brand babble that has confused customers and cost marketers money.

So, it may be better today to simply abandon the term *relationship* because it has become so contaminated. Maybe bonding or connections or some other term will better describe the linkage between the buyer and the seller. Software packages don't do it for either party. That's already been proven in the marketplace.

What about a Zipper?

How can we think about connecting customers and marketers through some type of approach that defines and illustrates the ongoing bonds between them. One we like originated by Vectia, in Finland. It's called the "Zipper."

The basic concept of the "Zipper" is that it connects the marketer and the customer. It starts with the marketer trying to understand what benefits and values the customer wants and needs. In the Finnish version, they phrase it as "How does the customer create value for him or herself?" That simply means trying to understand how the consumer solves problems, fills needs, satisfies wants, and so on. By knowing this, the marketer then tries to align his or her offerings or solutions or people or whatever to help the customer create that value. In short, it's a demand-oriented approach that enables the marketer and the brand to provide value based on what customers want and need, not what the marketing organization has available or wants to sell.

But, hang on a minute, you're likely saying. We've got a plant

Exhibit 6.1

SHIFTING THE BUSINESS FOCUS

Product-oriented thinking
"Old map"

"Where can we find customers for our products?"

Products — Price! — Customers

Traditional marketing

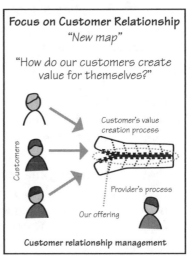

Focus on Customer Relationship
"New map"

"How do our customers create value for themselves?"

Customers

Customer's value creation process

Provider's process

Our offering

Customer relationship management

Source: Vectia Ltd.

that is making widgets in two colors and we're cranking out 3,000 an hour. We've got to have some people buying those widgets because we can't eat them. We've got to sell them to someone or face financial ruin.

All true. But, if this is the problem you face, you've got branding mixed up with business models. The babblers won't tell you that, but we will. Brands can only build relationships with people who have a need for the basic value proposition the brand offers. Don't fall into the trap of thinking branding is the solution to all your business problems. It isn't.

Rationalizing the Brand

So, let's be frank. One of the problems with the "Zipper" or any other brand relationship approach is that the marketer must rationalize the brand's customer base. There are only a certain number of customers whose interests, desires, requirements, and so on can be filled by the brand. Hard to believe, but there are still people in the world who don't, won't, or can't drink Coca-Cola.

Thus, the idea that the marketer can create a brand for "everyone" quickly goes out the window. Certain brands are for certain people. That's hard for most marketers to accept. Because the power to select and choose is increasingly in the hands of the customer or consumer, the marketer must be clear about who a brand is intended for and why they might like it. Customers choose the brands they want to be affiliated with. Marketers must make the brand available to be chosen.

And, that brings us to an interesting conundrum: If the marketer wants the brand to grow, he or she has only a few choices:

1. Find more people who accept what the brand is and how it operates in the marketplace. In other words, expand the customer base with like-minded prospects who will find value in the brand as it is. This can be done through communication, that is, introducing the brand to a wider audience. Or it can also mean expanding beyond the traditional geographic boundaries to find similar customers in other regions.

2. Change or alter the brand or brand communication so that it will appeal to more people. This can be done by improving

David Metzger

Decisions . . . decisions . . . decisions . . .
What is the best way to develop your brand's base?

quality and developing new associations and attributes that open the brand to new audiences. That's what Burberry's, MasterCard, and Harley Davidson did with tremendous results. However, such tinkering with the brand can be dangerous and may alienate current customers while failing to attract new ones in sufficient numbers. In recent years we have seen too many organizations—for example, almost all of the GM marques, Burger King, Kmart, and most of the regional telcos—that seem to be in a perpetual state of re-branding in an attempt to gain and retain customers, with little long-term effect. Maybe their problems aren't branding at all. But, try telling that to the branding experts who are advising them.

3. "Stretch the brand" into new but related areas. Cuisinart was able to extend its equities as the leading manufacturer of food processors into a cookware line. Vaseline extended its associations with extreme moisturizing capabilities into a line of hand and body lotions (Vaseline Intensive Care). The challenge is to find extensions that are relevant in order to

leverage core associations of the brand while not undermining or diluting it. Tricky business, that, with probably lots more failures than successes. We'll discuss the challenges of brand extensions further in Chapter 10.

4. Come up with a completely different brand to serve customer segments or channels the primary brand cannot or should not go after. For example, L'Oréal sells its high-end Lancôme line through fashionable department stores, and another, lower-priced L'Oréal line through grocery stores and drug stores. Such "stealth" brands allow the manufacturer to have offerings at several price points. It works, but it must be done carefully to avoid confusion and cannibalization between different customer segments and channel systems.

Regardless of which macro strategy you choose, the end result must be the same: to create and sustain an ongoing relationship or "bond" between the brand and a sufficient number of customers for it to be profitable and to provide you with an acceptable rate of return. Remember, the brand is supposed to make money for the owner, not just provide social "feel-goods."

In summary, brand relationships can be simple or complex. But in any and every case, they must be profitable to make the time and financial investment worthwhile for you, the brand owner.

Hopefully, someday, the brand babblers will understand this key point.

7

How to Avoid the
Mental Model
Minefields

𝖆s discussed in previous chapters, almost all advertising and communication concepts are based on some type of psychological model rather than on a business or financial base. That is, the historical focus of advertising and communication research has been on trying to understand how people take in, store, manage, and use information to find solutions to their wants and needs, solve their problems, enhance their lives and the like. Thus, because branding mavens have drawn so heavily on advertising and communication theory (sometimes to their benefit but often to their detriment), much of what they have researched, written, discussed, and, yes, babbled about brands and branding has been based on these same psychological models.

The whole area of Positioning makes the point.

The initial problem is that Positioning, like so many other marketing communication concepts and terms, has many meanings. For example, "branding experts" babble about a brand's market position. They babble about its position on the store shelf. They babble about finding an "unassailable brand position against competitors."

Or they babble about positioning the brand in the mind of the consumer.

Thus, Positioning has become one of the most overused, mis-used, and mis-understood terms in marketing communication. That raises the basic question:

Is Positioning, as it has and is being used in branding work, just another baseless concept, simply intuition revisited, or a valuable and useful tool?

Positioning: Problem Solver or Problem Maker?

Positioning, as it has been developed over the past twenty or so years, has created as many branding problems as it has solved. Many of the problems revolve around the multiple uses of the term as shown above. The other is that the concept is based on a now-dis-counted notion of how the human mind works.

Positioning, as it was initially envisioned, was based on a stimulus-response model of the human mind, that is, a relatively simple psychological model. In the late 1960s and early 1970s (seems like there was a lot going on then, doesn't it?), many psycho-logical models compared the human brain to the structural compo-nents of a computer, that is, a path-driven system that used menus and instructions for direction and assembly, with slots or spaces in the brain where concepts and ideas were stored.

Thus, the initial Positioning approach suggested there was a slot or location in the brain for everything, including products, services, and brands. Through advertising or other marketing and marketing communication activities, the marketer could fill those slots in the consumer's mind with their brands. By doing that, the marketer and the brand were unassailable. Fill the mental slot and no other brand could enter. Nor could the brand and product connection be dis-placed: There was no "erase" function in these mental models. Thus, the marketer was guaranteed the "brand slot" or "brand position" as long as the consumer was alive and thinking. And, not just any con-sumer, most all consumers. No wonder marketing people fell in love with the positioning idea.

Positioning was a really neat concept. Capture "the slot" in the human mind with advertising and marketing communication by

David Metzger

Mental Model Minefields

positioning the brand there and have a customer for life. Who wouldn't buy into this concept? Spend a few bucks, fill the mental "niche," and reap the rewards . . . forever.

It fit right in with the other concepts of the time. Mass advertising. Continuous repetition with television commercials. (Remember Anacin's "pounding hammers" or Mr. Whipple's continuous whining "Please don't squeeze the Charmin"?), almost ubiquitous product distribution and some type of minor technological or product "innovation" that gave the brand its "talking points." It's easy to see why Positioning was accepted, almost without question, as one of the basic elements in most advertising consultants' and brand gurus' toolboxes.

The problem was: The positioning concept was based on the then-current, but, now "old," psychology of Pavlov, Skinner, Maslow and others of the early and mid-twentieth century, not on the more recent approaches that rely on cognition, neural networks, multitasking, and the like.

So, when we didn't know any better, Positioning made a lot of sense.

And, lots of advertising, communication, and, yes, what were later to emerge as branding concepts, were based on these same historic premises: slots, niches, capturing "mind share" or "mind positions" and so on.

You still see and hear a lot about positioning from the brand babblers even today, although most of the concepts were dis-proven years ago. Simple, easy-to-use concepts where the marketer is in total control of the system die hard in the halls of babble-dom.

Networks, Not Niches

We now know, as was discussed in Chapter 5, that the brain is a network of loosely related concepts, ideas, experiences and the like that are constantly changing, being re-arranged, distorted, adapted, brought back together, reorganized and the like. Information and experiences are continuously being added and connected and networked in every person's mind. There aren't any "slots" to be filled. There aren't any "crevices" in which brands can be located. And, most of all, there aren't any "assigned seats" for products and services. If there were, Dell would never have ousted IMB, HP, and Toshiba as the largest selling small computer. Lexus would never have beaten up on Mercedes. And Southwest Airlines would never have succeeded against American and Continental and United. Brand positions are not forever. They're only for as long as something better hasn't yet arrived.

Positioning may be a good way for brand owners to "think and dream about" brands and branding. But, for practical applications and making money, it's sadly lacking. Cognitive science today says the basic premise behind positioning just isn't right. Like the Hierarchy of Effects and DAGMAR models, Positioning sounds really good when presented with slides and charts and graphs and lots of selected examples. It's brand babble at its finest. But, it's filled with holes and massive opportunities to spend money and get nothing back.

Taking Your Eye Off the Ball

As a brand planning thought process, Positioning does force the marketing communication community to give some thought to the relationship of the brand to other brands in the marketplace. And, it requires the discipline to establish what is unique or differentiating about a brand. So it does require an external view. That's good. But, that's also bad. Too frequently, it often generates another one of the "cardinal sins" of brand babbling: It moves attention away from customers and value creation and financial returns to the firm and puts it primarily on competitors, what they are doing, how they are marketing, what their advertising is and so on. Interesting, but only from an observational standpoint. Competitors can't make you money. Customers can.

The biggest problem with Positioning, as it has developed, been preached and mis-applied and practiced is that it is another one of those internally focused, navel-gazing routines that prevents marketers from focusing on people and profits. Again, brands are successful because people buy the brand or brands, not because you, as the brand marketer, have "outflanked" the competition or "seized the slot" or whatever the current positioning phrase is. People buy products and services. People buying products and services are what create sales and profits. So, back to the common theme: The things that are the most important in brands and branding are your customers and, to a certain extent, your employees. People as humans, not as computer slots and certainly not as functional units in a grand branding scheme.

Unfortunately, the practice of Positioning, at least the way the many babblers have developed it over the past decade, forces the marketing, sales, distribution, logistics, and all the other customer-facing people to focus on competitors, not on customers. How do we position against competitor A? What's our Positioning against the generics? What can we do about the brand position XYX brand has taken? All internal and all mostly irrelevant.

Brand Babble and Weather Forecasting

There's nothing wrong with understanding competitors. In fact, it's a good thing. But, from a brand's standpoint, it's often immaterial. The reason? You can't do anything about what your competitors do any more than you can do anything about the weather. It's nice to know when to bring along galoshes, but that doesn't stop the rain from falling.

Too many branding people have gotten too tangled up in too much brand babble about competitive Positioning. Who are our competitors? What are they saying? Have they left a hole in the Positioning map? Can we reposition them? Is there an unfilled niche? Can we outspend them? And on and on and on.

Internal focus to support an external system commonly just doesn't work.

If Positioning Is Bad, What's Good?

Is there a better way to think about how a brand might find its place in the sun? We think so.

To do that, we need to go back a few years and resurrect an old concept that has gotten lost in all the new babbling about consumers, communication, and, most of all, information processing, i. e., how people take in, manage, store and use information about a brand.

Our story starts with a researcher named Richard Vaughn, who at the time was employed by the Foote, Cone & Belding advertising agency. Vaughn challenged the basic "hypodermic" approach to advertising effects that had come from propaganda research in World War II and the work of other gurus who continued in that vein. Working during the late 1980s and early 1990s, Vaughn developed a concept that still has resonance and value today.

At the time of Vaughn's work, the belief was that if the advertiser or marketer injected the consumer or customer enough times with the same message, that information would have an effect on those exposed, i. e., they would rush to the store and buy the advertised product or brand. They couldn't help themselves. Pretty much the same theme and argument the Hierarchy of Effects and DAGMAR guys (circa 1960) had used earlier. (Recall our discussion in Chapter 4.)

Vaughn argued that rather than looking at how marketers viewed brands, it was the customer that really mattered. It was how they took in the brand messages—stored, recalled and used them—that was key. While Vaughn started with some of the same concepts the positioning gurus used, he argued for using communication in a different way. Rather than use the static concept that a brand fills a

Exhibit 7.1

THE "THINK, FEEL, DO" MODEL

	Thinking	Feeling
High Improvement	1. Informative (thinking) Model: think-feel-do Products: car, house Creative: demonstration, specific details	2. Affective (feeling) Model: feel-think-do Products: jewelry, cosmetics Creative: execution impact
Low Improvement	3. Habit formation (doing) Model: do-think-feel Products: liquor, household items Creative: reminder	4. Self-satisfaction (reacting) Model: do-feel-think Products: cigarettes, liquor, candy, gum Creative: attention

niche in the customer's brain and stays there forever, he used a cognitive approach. That approach suggested the consumer was an active participant in the marketing communication process. Thus, customers are dynamic and use different methods to process information about different types of products and services. As a result, consumers and customers have multiple ways of thinking about, considering, making decisions, and applying those decisions to multiple products and services over time and certainly, to brands.

In short, Vaughn argued that it was *how* consumers processed information that was really important, not how many messages were sent or how much "tonnage" the marketer used in his media program. Using this approach, he turned these concepts into a neat way to think about brand communication. (Actually, Vaughn didn't relate his concept specifically to branding, as he was focused on advertising. We did that. But, his work provides a really cool way to think about brands and brand messages).

Exhibit 7.1 shows the original Vaughn matrix. There are four elements. The Y axis or those things along the side have to do with how important the product or service is to the consumer. High involvement means it is important and worth thinking about. Low involvement simply means the product or service or concept or idea or brand or whatever is not terribly important, and, therefore, the customer or consumer doesn't invest a lot of time or energy in search or consideration.

Across the top, the X axis, are two terms, thinking and feeling. These are the processes consumers or customers use to make decisions. Thinking means they choose between alternatives, consider the decision, and so on. Feeling means they rely more on their emotions or how they "feel" about things the decision leads in this sequence. So, as shown, the matrix compares and contrasts thinking and feeling in both high-involvement and low-involvement products or services. This creates the four-box matrix in the illustration: (a) think-feel-do, (b) feel-think-do, (c) do-think-feel and (d) do-feel-think. All are different ways consumers and customers come into a brand consideration situation. It's not mechanical slots or niches or crevices they are using, it is rational thinking or their emotional alternatives.

So, study the chart and then relate your product or service or brand to one of the four boxes shown. Clearly, some brand situations are think-feel-do, others are do-think-feel and still others are feel-think-do. The key is which is relevant for your brand and for your customers.

In our view, the "Think-Feel-Do" approach Vaughn developed provides a much better way to develop an outside-in approach to brand communication than do the old-line positioning approaches that seem to assume all customers and all consumers and all products and all services are essentially the same and that all your brand is doing is "filling a slot" in their heads by jamming messages down their throats.

So, the next time the babblers start talking about their "model," ask them what underlies it? Having the "think-feel-do" and the other models in your mind will generally help you cut through the nonsense.

Customer Insights Win, Positioning Loses

In the brand babble arena, the Vaughn matrix of how consumers go about considering various products, services, and brands seems to make much more sense than the competitor-oriented concepts of Positioning. While there are some good reasons to use a Positioning approach when developing a brand—e.g., for example trying to displace Wal-Mart as the lowest price mass merchandiser with a corner store on the outskirts of Rahway, New Jersey, with only your poverty-stricken uncle's resources to influence the market—the entire approach, with its almost single-minded focus on competition, and not consumers, generally creates more confusing brand babbling than insight for the brand owner.

Understanding how customers think about, consider, capture, and store information and the pathways they might take to understand your brand is a much more relevant way of developing a "brand understanding" than the simplistic approaches of positioning. Cognitive processing at least recognizes the current state of psychology and how humans process and store information in their minds. So, at least your brand thinking is based on what your customers actually think, feel, and do.

So, you might want to start with customers when developing or maintaining your brand rather than your competitors. And, you might want to question what the babblers mean when they start down the "positioning" path with your brand or brands. You can dump a lot of cash into positioning maps and still not know very much.

Our next stop on this brand sojourn is understanding how brands appear, the look or looks they take on, and the like. Most likely, that has something to do with the success of the brand. Read the next chapter and find out.

8

Magic Words, Mystic Signs, and Other Mind-bending Concepts

Probably no group has been more responsible for the development of brand babble over the past 20 or so years than the so-called "creatives." Those same groups have also been primarily responsible for developing some of the most relevant brand concepts as well. "Creatives" are both a blessing and a curse for brand owners: They cost a lot of money, but they can sometimes make you a lot of money. Obviously, the problem for brand managers and owners, then, is separating "good" creative from "bad" creative or, better said, the brand developers from the brand charlatans.

And, that's not easy.

Creative is terribly subjective, particularly when it is applied to the areas of product development, naming, design, packaging, graphics, colors, electronic imaging, film, video, and all the other tools of the creative trade. It's closely related to and dependent on culture, background, and, yes, even the taste of those developing the "creative product." And those judging it as well. Thus, it's difficult for senior management to say "I like what they have done" and say why or, more important, "I don't like what they have done and here are the specific reasons." Subjectivity, pure and simple.

But, there is a key point here. The money the "creatives" plan on spending is not theirs, it's yours. The risk that is being taken is by you and your organization, not by them. Keep that always in mind: Creatives love toys, and they love to spend other people's money, and they worry very little about whether or not their recommendations "work" in the marketplace. If they're pleased with the "output," you should be pleased with the "outcome," whether you got a nickel of your money back or not.

So, how can one cut through all the brand babble that usually accompanies the presentations made by the people dressed in black? How does one determine what is good for the brand, what is bad for the brand, and what is simply creative expression on a rampage?

Ah, the joys of subjectivity!

Getting a Grip on Creativity

To get a grip on the "creativity" issue, we reflect back on what Stan Tannenbaum, one of the great copywriters and creative directors of the last half of the twentieth century and a member of the Northwestern University IMC faculty for more than 15 years, said. He described the process as "controlled creativity." By that, he meant that the creative implementation should always be focused on the product or service being promoted and on the customers and consumers who would hopefully be influenced. The "creative product" was not and should not be focused on the communication elements or activities being used in the promotional program. In Stan's words, "it wasn't creative unless it sold something to someone."

Being creative, simply for the sake of being creative or attention-getting was, in his view, the anathema of modern advertising, marketing communication, and branding.

And Stan was right. Brands are developed for only two reasons: to benefit the brand owner and to benefit the brand user. Even though Andy Warhol made the Campbell soup can famous as a "creative expression," the Campbell Soup Company didn't go into the soup business to provide fodder for Warhol's artistic endeavors. They went into the soup business to sell soup, provide nourishment for hungry Americans, and make some money along the way. Or in the words of Huntley Baldwin, former creative vice president at Leo Burnett and one of the major participants in the development of all the cute characters in Keebler and Jolly Green Giant commercials: "We buy artwork. We are not patrons of the arts."

So, the first question to ask in any evaluation of the creative elements of the brand and branding efforts is: Does it help build the brand and help sell the product? If it doesn't, start to quickly look elsewhere for if you don't, you'll soon find yourself in a creative whirlpool accused of "not understanding creative work" or "not knowing what is current or mod" or even worse, "a nuts-and-bolts fascist who is trying to stifle creative expression." It's that last one that should give you the real key to what is controlled creativity and what is simply some creative person trying to satisfy his or her own whims and ego.

Always remember: It's your brand and your money, and, most likely, you want to sell products and keep customers happy, not enhance or glorify the whims of a "creative."

In the twenty or more years we have been trying to understand, build, and maintain brands, five basic lessons about brands and creativity have emerged. We call them the "Bewares." You'll see why in the following sections.

Beware the Lure of Attention

Creative people love attention. That's why they dress the way they do. It's why they have purple hair, use iridescent makeup, and do all the other "creative" things they do. They love to be the center of the stage, in the spotlight, even if people in the back rows are snickering. In short, they love attention.

And, they basically believe brands love or should love attention. They often believe the old saw that "any publicity, no matter how damning, is good publicity."

Wrong. Bad publicity is bad publicity. End of another story.

Thus, some creative people believe in "shock value." That is, getting attention at any price. Crude. Lewd. Lascivious. Push the envelope. It's all the same to them. Remember, these are the guys who thought paying $2.1 million to buy thirty seconds of time during the 2000 Super Bowl was a great stratagem. And who, only a few months earlier, thought shooting gerbils out of a cannon was really "creative" and would "get attention" and create "industry buzz." It did at the time, but do you remember who the advertiser was or the point of the "creative"? How far did this go in building a sustainable brand, one that engenders respect and commitment and most of all, a willingness to trade money for the brand offering?

Clearly, one of the great uses of creativity for a brand over the years has been Apple. While you might argue with their business model, Apple's use of "controlled creativity" in building a brand has been incredible. From the "1984" commercial to the Apples for Schools program to the new "see-through desktop," Apple has been on the cutting edge of creativity. But all with a purpose. To sell more Apple computers to get more people involved in the "Apple approach to computing."

So, the first "beware" is beware of attention for attention's sake. Controlled creativity is the goal.

Beware the Herd of Sheep

In Chapter 3, we talked about separating brands from fads and fashions. The same is true for brand communication. The entire field of advertising, marketing, marketing communication, and brands and branding, in particular, is that it is one of the most copy-cat and lemming-like realms in all of business.

While most people involved in brands and branding extol creativity, argue vehemently about it, and believe they are paragons of new thinking and new direction, most of them are like a herd of sheep. Have one commercial or one ad or one brand communication concept break out of the pack and every creative person and his cadre of associates will copy it—almost to the letter (or as close as they can get to replicating it without being sued). If copying is the most sincere form of flattery, then the creatives are the greatest flatterers ever.

Once a breakthrough concept, such as the "critters" that Leo Burnett was so adept at creating for Kellogg and Keebler and Pillsbury and Green Giant, worked, every branding creative was hot on the trail of another, more loveable critter. Once Dave Thomas became the likeable "spokesperson" for Wendy's, every other branding company that had an owner or general manager or CEO who could read his lines without stumbling showed up as a brand spokesperson. (Remember the Ford CEO during the Firestone controversy?) And what about the beer guys? Can you really have a beer brand without showing a slow-motion pour while someone extols the virtues of the brand in dulcet tones. And the list could go on interminably.

Today, brands must stand for something—something inherently relevant and compelling to the customer. Not something borrowed or stolen from a competitor. Not something that registers just because it jars or violates sensitivities or damages the ear drum. Brands should stand for something and that something must be something that will endure, not just fly high and then crash with a thud.

So, the second "beware" in branding is to ask if it is really new or if it is simply something borrowed or something blue (as in off-taste, not the color). If so, ask the creatives to try again. They won't like you, but, remember, it is your money that is at risk, not theirs.

Beware the Explanation

Too many times, branding and brand communication are sold by creatives to brand managers and owners through some type of "explanation." The creatives "explain": "You won't really understand what we are doing so let us explain it a bit." Then they take you through the process, the symbolism, the most current "new wave" or "new era" or "new whatever" design or technique, patiently explaining how hip or hop or mod or clever what they have done is. At the end, they expect you to raise them on your shoulders and carry them triumphantly from the room to the cheers of the accompanying throngs. Great creative. Great brand communication.

Maybe.

But probably not.

Two things are generally going on here.

One, if you are so out of touch with your brand audience that the "creative" must be explained to you, then you can't make a reasonable decision anyway. So abdicate the responsibility. Give them the money. Set up a meeting with your banker in case it doesn't work and move on.

Or, second, if the brand communication really requires explanation, ask the simple question: "Who is going to explain this to our brand audience?" Given today's short attention spans, interactive and networked audiences that have grown up on sound bites and electronic bytes won't wait for the explanation. They'll be gone. And so will your brand investment. The only thing you'll likely get back will be the bills for the "creative."

So, if the brand message needs explaining or the brand concept needs "talking through," explain to the creatives that explanation is not on the agenda for most customers or prospects today. That's the third "beware."

In short, brand messages must be incredibly short. Incredibly clear. Incredibly easy to understand. Take a look at Evian: mountains and clear, sparking water. Take a look at Altoids: curiously strong. Backed up by the product. Take a look at UPS: "What can Brown do for you today?" Or their competitor, FedEx: "When it absolutely, positively has to be there." All of these are clear, concise, with no explanation needed.

And, no creative tagging along to "explain what the brand is" or "what the brand message is" or "what the brand meaning is" either.

So, demand creativity that needs no explanation. There's no time for it in today's world.

Beware the "Mini-Movie" Makers

Stuffed away in the bottom drawer of the desk of many creative people is a rough draft for a movie script. Too many "creatives" are only serving time in branding and brand communication, waiting for an opportunity to meet Steven Spielberg or Quentin Tarrantino, or Spike Lee . . . on your money. Their real goal is to make movies or epics or creative statements on film or video. And you, the brand owner, are their passport to fame and fortune.

What these guys really want is to make a piece of film or video that they can "put on their reel," not necessarily to help you sell products or services and certainly not to help customers understand and build relationships with your brand. While there aren't a lot of these guys and gals out there, there are enough of them to put up the "Beware" sign when they come around.

How can you tell whether your "creative people" are interested in your brand, or simply making a short epic that will be recognized and lionized (as in the Cannes Film Festival, the nirvana of all "creatives"). Ask a few simple questions:

"Why do you think people should buy or use or enjoy our brand?"

If the answers tend to focus on the creative material they have just shown you, take a hike.

Or ask: "What do you think is the underlying value proposition of our brand to customers and prospects?" If you get a blank stare, close your wallet and walk away.

Or if when asked: "What type of financial returns will this 'creative effort' return to us?" they start to talk about ratings and awards and industry talk and "street buzz," put on your business face and head for the door

This is not meant to denigrate good, solid creative work by dedicated "creative people." The film genre has been undoubtedly advanced by the BMW mini-movies, a real breakthrough in a creative sense in an era of "one-liners." It is meant simply to help you separate the "creatives-interested-in-you-and-your-brand" from "creatives-interested-in-their–own-careers-and-building–their-reels–with-your-money."

So who does great cinema for brands? Look at what Anheuser-Busch has done with the Clydesdales over the years. Mini-movies? Sure. But, with a real heart-warming, *relationship-building, brand-building* message. Or look at what MasterCard has done with their "Priceless" theme. Slice-of-life? Yeah. Memorable? For sure. Effective in differentiating the brand? One of the best.

So, the fourth "beware" is: Beware the extra cost, extra elements, extra location and extra personality creatives. Most likely they want to line their pockets with your brand exposure.

Beware the Obfuscation of Design

Most of us are pretty good at understanding design. We commonly can tell which types of architecture we like and why. We can generally explain our preferences in art and painting. We know which colors, when put together in the wrong way, are jarring. And we can even tell whether or not the design of the logotype goes with the brand it is to represent. But, if that is the case, why are we so "buffalo-ed" when we get in a room of brand designers?

Colors and typefaces and placement on the page seem to confuse and confound even the most senior managers. We end up approving things that won't fit on the page or won't reproduce on paper or even the plastic we use for our packaging. Or we realize three days after all the stationery is printed that we hate the design and colors and can't read the lettering on the business cards.

Most of us who deal with brands and branding have been there and done that. The question is why?

The chief culprit is the big screen, the close-up cameras and the soothing tones of the brand designer. As in the "Beware" #2 above, the explanation tends to lull us into submission.

We were sitting in a brand redesign presentation with a client a number of years ago. After spending weeks rummaging through the company looking for just the right "feel and tone" to take the brand forward into a new era of success, when it came time to present the new design, senior management was astonished to see that it was the same logo, the same colors, the same type face, in short, it looked like nothing had been done. Then the design team "explained." They had connected the R and the D in the corporate name to reflect the new organizational emphasis on Research and Development. While they agreed that the change was subtle, they were sure that consumers and employees would see the connection and that it would create a radically new image for the company.

What wasn't so subtle in the process was the price tag. Several hundreds of thousands of dollars to "hook the R and the D together." On a big screen, it made some sense. On a small package, it looked like a printing error.

So, the final Beware is "Beware the design gurus who have to change something just to justify their fees."

Good idea.

There are, of course, other "bewares" but if you follow these five, you can stand your own with the "creatives." They deserve repeating:

1. Beware the Lure of Attention. (Beware of attention for attention's sake.)
2. Beware the Herd of Sheep. (Beware of trend trackers: Ask if it is simply something borrowed or something blue [as in off-taste, not the color].)
3. Beware the Explanation. (The brand message must be

David Metzger

*. . . But if you look at it from over here,
it looks like a big turnip . . .*

incredibly short. If it needs explaining or a concept "talking through," it already misses the point.)
4. Beware the "Mini-Movie" Makers. (Beware the extra cost, extra elements, extra location and extra personality creatives.)
5. Beware the Obfuscation of Design. (Beware the design gurus who change something just to justify their fees.)

Next, another look at culture and backgrounds as we consider the globalization of brands in Chapter 9.

9

Going Global

About thirty years ago, Marshall McLuhan, the peripatetic Canadian communications expert, predicted the development of a global village. Many people scoffed.

But today that global village is here. The Internet, satellite TV, advanced telephony systems, trade agreements, continuous securities trading, and the like are facilitating global and even some extra terrestrial communication and commerce. That means all brands have become, de facto, global brands, simply because information for and about them is increasingly available, globally.

Now, don't get excited. The mere fact of globalization doesn't mean every brand is going to see global sales. But, it does mean that every brand is competing in a global marketplace. Against global, not just local competitors, whether they are clearly visible or not.

So, while there's truth in this "all brands are global" sound bite, it likely doesn't fully explain the options and challenges facing today's brand managers and brand owners. The key question continues: Where and in what way are you going to make money with your brand or brands.

Certainly, with the scope and capabilities of electronic communication, any product, service, thing, or even body can be recognized and even known around the world. While the local pizza shop may not have intended it, its web site can be accessed in Beijing or Kiev, just as readily as Hometown, USA. Obviously, the pizza guy would have great difficulty delivering pizzas to Beijing or Kiev. But it's certainly feasible that the Hometown brand of pizza could be accessed and known by Internet surfers anywhere.

The big difference in brand thinking today is this: It's not where the brand is sold that counts, it's where the brand is known. And what the brand is known for and at what level. That's the key to brand management in the twenty-first century.

That means it's more difficult to continue the traditional, and generally very profitable, multinational branding practices of previous times. That includes such things as having different pricing, labeling, packaging, and communication on a country-by-country basis. Communication simply doesn't follow borders anymore. Thus, today and tomorrow, brands will continue to be challenged to become more consistent and more unified in their operations and activities, everywhere. The idea of a "global look, with a local flavor" or, as it is sometime referred to as "glocal," will increasingly become the rule.

Hung Up in the Past

The real branding problem in today's global or glocal marketplace? Too much focus on the 4Ps. Brand babbling from the past, focused on product, price, promotion, and, particularly, place (distribution). Interesting, but all internally focused and all structured to what the organization can and wants to do. The question, of course: What kind of reciprocal benefits can occur in this type of "marketer first" atmosphere? Not many.

4Ps reasoning says if you can't physically distribute in an area, you can't be relevant. Not true. Today, if you're important enough to them, people will find out about you and come to you. Just look at the visitor list at Disney World.

Or, the babblers say, if the product is too high-end (or too low-end) for a market, just reposition and reprice it to adapt to local realities. Again, not true. You simply can't market in isolation given today's communication landscape. Nor can you "over-market" your product around the world. Izod almost killed their brand through proliferation a number of years ago. They've been struggling to rebuild the alligator icon ever since.

How you answer the globalization question has a lot to do with your future success both here and abroad, if there really is an "abroad" anymore.

Globalization Today

The idea of globalization was first verbalized by Harvard's Ted Levitt in the 1980s. Back then there were few examples he could reference. He was, as you might expect, chastised by various "international experts" (notice we said "international," not "global" experts).

When Levitt first proposed "globalization," the brand babblers said the concept of "global"—having a unified, consistent presence around the world—was only a theory, a pipedream that could never happen in the actual marketplace. Cultures, local customs, government regulations, distribution systems and even communication channels, they claimed, were just too locally developed to ever permit global brands to exist.

So, they argued for a "multinational" perspective, i.e., the development of brands on a national market basis, sold locally through a market-by-market implementation approach. In other words, the status quo.

Remember, those were the days when governments controlled the flow of goods into and out of their countries. Even in Europe, France and Belgium were separated by the "invisible border" of customs, duties and regulations and even communication systems. Almost every large marketing organization was based on developing a national or tightly defined regional unit, one for Germany, one for the United Kingdom, one for Scandinavia, and so on. Therefore, the country manager was king, and he or she did not recognize anyone or anything outside their own borders, except maybe the CEO when he arrived for the annual visit.

So, when Levitt was writing, there were "multinational marketers and brands," that is, organizations that marketed in multiple countries but practically none in a global way. It just wasn't possible.

But, technology, communication systems and, most of all, diplomacy and the need to develop relevant markets forced governments and marketers to create global alliances such as the European Union, MERCOSUR, NAFTA, and others. Today, globalization is real although some marketers and some theoreticians still don't recognize it. They babble on about localization.

David Metzger

The Reality of Brand "Architecture"

So, global brands are here and yours may be one of them whether you recognize it or not and whether you want it to be or not. The challenge is how to organize around it and how to make sure it's not undermined by the regional or national centers of power.

Developing Local, Transnational, and Global Brands

Brands can be classified on three levels, depending on the market and the marketer's strategy.

One, local brands are developed specifically for individual or geographically limited markets. Local brands are sold primarily in a specific city, state, or country. Examples would be Eli's Cheesecake, an institution in Chicago, or Victoria Bitter, the most popular beer in

Australia, but sold almost entirely within the country's borders. Each represents an offering where commonality of language, understanding of tastes, heritage, customs, and culture enable the brand to use locally recognizable icons, and symbols.

These brands may have limited distribution beyond their home market and may take on a certain exotic cachet when distributed in other regions. However, they're always closely defined by their origins and local characteristics. Generally, this limits their appeal to larger, external markets. Thus, Vegemite will likely always be a quintessentially Australian brand, even though it has distribution in other countries. And it is unlikely Ambassador cars will find a substantial role in the automotive market outside of India.

Two, transnational brands are offered in multiple regions under a common brand name, but with significantly different pricing, distribution, or brand identity strategies. For example, the Lean Cuisine sold in Australia has substantially different packaging, logo design, menu choices, and caloric content then its American counterpart. Similarly, Pizza Hut in China has a far different menu, with wider choices and a higher level of service than in its US home market. Holiday Inn represents a much higher level of hostelry in Europe and Asia than in the US. Each of these brands has been extensively adapted to take advantage of local customs, tastes, expectations, and opportunities.

This isn't bad, but it does mean the internationalized versions are often unrecognizable to customers from the home market. To the extent that customers are crossing borders (physically or electronically) and expecting consistency in the offering, there can be a disconnect. This is generally not a problem for food brands, (see above) but it can create a thornier issue for others such as financial services, apparel, pharmaceuticals, technology, and business-to-business brands, where product and marketing consistency is expected.

Three, global brands cross boundaries easily, leveraging their popularity in one region into another and doing so while maintaining a unified and consistent identity. Brands such as Coca-Cola, Ikea, and Heineken come to mind as obvious examples, but there are many others. Technology and B-to-B brands such as IBM, HP, and Caterpillar are global brands, as are most international airlines and hotels like the Hyatt, Four Seasons, and Mandarin Oriental groups. MTV is a global brand, for it represents a fast-rising global culture and lifestyle that is as relevant in Thailand as in Texas. CNN, too, is a global brand based on its 24-hour news coverage. The same might be said for Carrefour, the fast-growing French retailer that is as much at home in Chile as in Courvesin.

Importantly, these global brands often adapt some aspects of their offering to local markets. For example, Coca-Cola is a global brand, but if you look at the product and the packaging, it's often localized. The Coke in China doesn't taste like or look like the one you see in India or the Philippines. Similarly, CNN has different news coverage in different regions, and is even beginning to offer broadcasts in languages other than English. But, in each of these examples, the core brand is the same worldwide. Same underlying concept. Same brand meaning and identity. Same customer value proposition.

This classification scheme is quite simple. If you're in charge of growing a brand across borders, your first job is to evaluate its global potential. Is the product or service too "local" to become a transnational or too "transnational" to become "global"? Is the opportunity for a transnational strategy sufficient to justify the expense of maintaining multiple (and potentially conflicting) brand strategies? Research is helpful. But not local research. You need research that provides a view of the widest possible area in which you plan to market. Our approach: Think global at the start because you never know how fast and how far your brand can and will go.

Product or Corporate Brand?

A related question is: How and in what way should the corporate brand be used in your branding strategy? Again, there are multiple choices. You can have a single, corporate brand used around the world, or you can rely on the corporate brand as an "endorser," that is, to give credibility to the brands. Or you can rely on product brands with no mention of the corporate parent. It all depends on what you are trying to do and how you view your organization. Exhibit 9.1 illustrates the differences between a "house brand" and a "house of brands" with many alternatives in the middle.

If your company started in Japan or Korea, this is a no-brainer. You use the corporate brand as much as possible and try to stretch it to cover a multitude of products and services the same way Sony, Samsung, Mitsubishi, and LG have done.

If you started in North America or Europe, you likely started with

Exhibit 9.1

BUILDING THE BRAND ARCHITECTURE

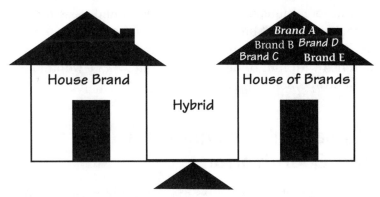

a product brand such as Omo or Tide or Persil. You hid the name of your parent company or if you used it at all, it was only as a passing reference. The product brand view, widely practiced and promulgated by the fast-moving-consumer-goods (fmcg) guys, has often subsumed the corporate brand. That view is changing. For example, both P&G and Unilever have been rationalizing their brand holdings. Selling off or closing long-term products. Why? They've learned that media proliferation, audience fragmentation, and retail consolidation and concentration have raised the cost of multi-brand marketing to a level that even their deep pockets cannot afford. Few, if any marketers today or tomorrow, can afford to offer an individual brand for every consumer desire.

Today, P&G is starting to "tag" their television commercials in Asia-Pacific with a corporate umbrella message, e.g., trying to tie all their disparate product lines together. In short, even the big guys can't afford multi-product branding today. They have to move to a corporate view to get greater synergy between the product brands and the overall umbrella brand. This is a big area for brand babblers. So be forewarned.

Is Corporate Branding for You?

The corporate branding issue raises many interesting questions: Can or should you use the corporate brand? Corporate brands have great

value among many constituencies, i.e., customers, employees, strategic partners, and, of course, the financial community. The problem:
The corporate brand is often "owned" or "controlled by" corporate
communication managers and groups, not brand-focused managers.
So, if you're a product brand manager, you need a new friend in the
future, the corporate communication manager. You may want to
share lunch with him or her, for you likely will be wanting to share
his or her corporate brand as well.

Endorsements, Alignments, and Coordination

Using the corporate brand raises another set of branding questions,
too. For example, if the corporate brand is to be used, how, when,
and where is that done? Brand babblers often make corporate and
product brand relationships as complicated as possible. They bring
in complex diagrams with dotted lines, solid boxes, shifting arrows,
all depicting what they call "brand architecture."

The relationship between the corporate and product or unit
brands doesn't have to be mysterious and complicated. It basically
boils down to three alternatives as shown in Exhibit 9.1.

One, monolithic corporate brands use the company name and
identity for all of their offerings, e.g., Nokia, Accenture, Four Seasons
Hotels, Starbucks. While there might be individual product offerings
under this name, the branding emphasis is solidly on the corporate
parent, and all design and identity elements focus on the organizational name and logo.

Two, corporate umbrella brands use the company name in con-
junction with all, or almost all, product or divisional brands. The corporate name may be in a primary role (e.g., Dell Inspiron) or a
secondary, endorsing role (Courtyard by Marriott). Similarly, the company may even exclude its corporate name when necessary. For example, General Electric has aggregated almost all their units under
corporate competency brands, GE Aircraft Engines, GE Plastics, GE
Appliances and the like, while leaving RCA and NBC relatively dis-
tinct and separate. A few years ago, Hewlett-Packard went through a
huge rebranding effort to shift emphasis from its individual printer
product lines (Ink Jet, Laser Jet, Desk Jet, and so on) and to link them
more closely to the HP label. Why? They learned the equities HP rep-

resented were uniquely differentiating and added value in what were becoming increasingly competitive and commoditized lines.

The corporate name can play an important endorsing role that unifies the brand portfolio and makes sure the product brands get full advantage of the association with the parent. For example, Post-it Notes gets additional value by being endorsed by 3M. Same for Scotchguard. And DuPont adds value to Lycra and Tivex. In truth, the linking of the corporate name to products is basically a question of value addition. And that is something that requires more than a neat graphic or a clever use of the two logos, no matter what the branding gurus might say.

Three, product brands put most of the emphasis on the individual product or service offering. Many product brands started in North America simply because many consumer goods marketers couldn't see beyond the American borders. But, when the Toyotas and Nestles and Canons and Panasonics of the world entered the US marketplace, product branders learned some important lessons. For one thing, these companies supported a wide range of product offerings under a single, broad corporate brand efficiently and effectively. And since support for individual product brands isn't getting any easier or any less expensive, you should consider consolidating your brands under fewer identities, particularly if you have wandered off into "product brand land," which is where so many brand managers want to be.

We're not saying there is never any value in product branding or that all brands must carry the corporate name. That's too pro-scriptive and too much like babbling. For example, there is often significant value in keeping the corporate brand in the background, particularly when it might detract from a specialized offering. For example, a prominent display of the Kraft brand would add little value to the up-market Gevalia Coffee or Altoids mint offerings. Kraft is there, but you have to look for it. And this is why GE has allowed NBC to maintain its own identity, rather than renaming it GE Broadcasting. Such strategies are generally the exception rather than the rule. One always has to recognize the additional costs, risks, and complexity involved when multiple brand levels are sustained.

With this discussion of global brands and some comments on the corporate-product brand issue, we can move to a logical extension, brand extensions. That's Chapter 10.

10

Birth Pains and Stretch Marks

Nowhere in branding is there more babble than in the terms, terminology, and techniques used to launch new brands, extend existing brands into new areas, or revitalize a tired old brand by stretching it into a different shape. It's a shame so much brand babbling goes on in this arena because the opportunity for profit for the brand owner is greater here than in almost anywhere else.

How do we know there is so much babble going on? Just look at the success rate of new consumer products and brands in the US. A longstanding industry rule of thumb says that fewer than 20 percent of the new products will succeed. The truth today may be far worse, as recent research conducted by Copernicus Marketing and Ernst & Young, as well as that conducted by Neilsen BASES, indicates. Those results indicate the success rate may in fact be as low as only 10 to 15 percent.[1] Yet, almost every one of those "brand bombs" generally went through what their managers considered to be a "rigorous screening, testing and development process."

But, if the system is so "rigorous," why do so many of those brands fail? Better yet, why do so few succeed?

Predicting the Future

The major problem is the babble surrounding a most imperfect and inexact approach to new brand launches. In terms of marketing and consumer behavior, the research tools being used simply don't work sufficiently well, given the stakes involved. The error rates are too high and the tolerance for mistakes is too great. And, the babble that protects the born losers is simply too loud to hear over.

For example, one of the most widely used methodologies to identify potential success in new products is a research technique called conjoint analysis, a fancy name for forced choice research. When "conjoint" is used to screen for new products, a batch of likely users is gathered. They are then asked to choose what they like or dislike about a product or a brand or a name or whatever. In other words, "Do you want a big one or a little one," "Would you pay $4 or $6 for this particular configuration?" Or "Which vacuum cleaner would you prefer: one that picks up cat hair or one that will pick up leaves and sticks?" (While these might sound ridiculous, these are the types of research questions often used.)

Based on the "choices" or "trade-offs" made by the research victims, decisions are made about product features, names, price levels, and everything in between. Forced choices by "not necessarily buying customers." No real commitment, particularly any commitment to lay money down on the counter in exchange for the product. No other requirement than for the respondent to give an opinion.

Please don't think we're picking on conjoint or any of the other raft of research or other statistical techniques used in new brand work. We're not. They all have the same problem. They're testing people and people's opinions. Most important, they're asking and relying on people to be able to tell the researchers what they might do in the future. In other words, they are requesting "attitudes and opinions and even projected behaviors" from people with little to no risk involved in their decisions. Then, they are asking people to project those opinions to time periods they have trouble dealing with or even imagining.

No wonder 80 to 95 percent of all new products fail. People just can't tell you what they might do in the future. They can recall the past, sometimes with a bit of accuracy. But, for predicting the future: that's a major shortcoming.

So, that's the first challenge. The research techniques we use to test and evaluate new brands, new brand names, new line extensions and new almost anything.

Success Comes in Threes

In truth, the success of a new brand is dependent on only three things: (1) Will people buy it the first time? (2) Will they repurchase it a second or third time? (3) Can it be sold at a sufficient price to cover costs and return a profit?

If you want to know this, in-market tests are the only real solution, albeit not a panacea. Yes, they're expensive, slow, and open to competitors' viewing, but about the only real way to really know if you have a success or a failure is testing in the marketplace among real, living, breathing customers. If you get to the second or third purchase among enough people to make the product or service worthwhile, you will probably have a brand success. If you don't, you'll at least have a warning of a brand failure. It's as simple as that. How consumers behave in the marketplace, not how they think or what they believe or, sadly enough, even what they say.

Having said that, we recognize that there are circumstances in which it is not physically or legally possible to conduct an in-market test. So there are times when there is no alternative but to rely on projective techniques. However, such tools must be used with caution and with the understanding that they have limited value for predicting what consumers might do or buy in the future.

Here's something else to ponder. If flawed research is so poor at predicting what launches will succeed, maybe they are just as bad at predicting which products will fail. How many aborted product ideas might have gone on to be financially successful but for the fact that their development did not get through a poorly conducted concept testing stage or an ill-conceived conjoint analysis?

Will It Stretch to Liberal, Kansas?

The second major area is brand extensions. Can you bring out other products under your current brand name or some version of it? Obviously, if you can use the same brand name to sell several products, that's real marketplace efficiency. You save time and money and get greater returns.

Lots of babble here as well. Extendability studies. Brand "stretching" exercises. Focus groups with a bunch of housewives on the outskirts of Milwaukee. All being asked the same questions: Would you buy a new type of mango-chili yogurt if we call it Dannon? How about if we called it Yoplait? Or what would you think if we put the name Uncle Ferd's Finest on it? You tell us what you think and the people behind the one-way mirror will project that to the universe.

You get the picture. How far can the brand stretch and what products would customers accept under the brand offered? Some of this makes sense. Can or would you believe that the fine folks at Dunkin' Donuts could make a cereal? Or that Campbell Soup could make a tomato sauce? Sure, the companies can *make* the products, but will people accept them? As it turned out, these companies learned the hard way that customers put limitations on what they will accept from the brand regardless of their manufacturing capabilities. Or, their brand and branding budgets.

In truth, most line extension questions are nothing more than a matter of good common sense. And, again, that's not to denigrate the research folks. It's simply the problem with people. The questions we're asking are being asked of people and people often simply don't know how or what they would or could or should do. So, sometimes they make up things. They want to make the researcher happy. They don't want to sound ignorant or stupid. They want to appear to be rational shoppers or buyers or whatever. But, in too many cases, they just don't know. That's the problem with people.

Is the Corporate Brand Elastic?

So, what's the answer to line extensions and brand stretching? Sometimes it is just better to give the product an entirely new name, perhaps reinforcing and supporting it with the values of the corporate brand. From our view, properly handled, the corporate brand

David Metzger

The limits of Brand "Elasticity"

can be stretched generally much further than product brands. The latter are usually highly specific and grounded in their brand physical attributes and established uses. This singularity of purpose and function may be a great asset for product brands in their current form, but they do provide barriers. Absolut is so closely associated with vodka and Sweden that it is unlikely the firm would want to or could introduce Absolut Gin or Absolut Rum. Nor do we expect Ragu to introduce a line of soy sauce.

Corporate brands, on the other hand, are often built on a broader platform of competence and experience that allows the brand to participate in several different related businesses. Thus the HP "umbrella" has been broadened over the years from its early association with optical wizardry and measurement devices to now cover printers, computers, organizers, information technology, and the spirit of invention.

Another example, one that has taken this principle of stretching to an extreme, is Virgin. Richard Branson has stretched the Virgin brand from record stores to colas to hotels and airlines. Of course, some say that Branson IS the Virgin brand, but therein may lie the point: The Virgin brand is not about expertise in any one field; it is about an outlook, a way of managing, a way of serving customers, a view of the world that people seem to like.

But a word of caution here. Corporate brands have their limits and they are not infinitely stretchable. It takes years of building a proper base before a brand can be successfully stretched, and even then it is not always wise to do so. In spite of a few missteps here and there, Disney has been brilliant in leveraging their brand, as have L'Oréal and Marriott. That is not to say that all corporate brands can be stretched or extended. To their credit, Starbucks has kept its brand clearly focused on coffee (even though they offer other refreshments and merchandise), and it would be hard to imagine Kikkoman producing anything other than soy sauce, or Harley Davidson making anything other than motorcycles.

Reputation and Trust, Reputation and Trust

As W.C. Fields used to say "brains and personality, my boy, brains and personality." We might adapt that to: "reputation and trust, my brand, reputation and trust," for that is what seems to be the basic ingredient in how a brand can be extended, a new brand introduced or how an existing brand might be recycled, relaunched or whatever.

Back to our example of Richard Branson. The public just seems captivated by his roguish, iconoclastic, "thumb-his-nose-at-the-establishment" ways. And they seem to trust him. So, if Sir Richard says, "I'm going into the telephone business, and I'm going to call the company Virgin and the brand Virgin," a number of people will say, "Let's give it a go if Richard is behind it and the name on it is Virgin."

And, staying in the UK for a moment, the same thing has happened with Tesco, the supermarket people. They have, over the past ten or so years, built an incredible loyalty to Tesco and everything Tesco does and stands for with its customers. With over eight million people in the UK carrying and using the Tesco loyalty card, called the "Tesco Clubcard," they have learned enough about their customers so that they know they can succeed in new ventures and new businesses even before they decide to expand or launch. That has allowed the company to move into the Internet grocery business and succeed where almost every other food store owner has failed. It allowed them to enter the financial services business with insurance and banking. It enabled them to enter the wine club and vacation club business. And it even has enabled them to succeed in the pet insurance business as well, something most people would have never predicted.

So, the third thought on brand launches and brand extensions is: If people don't trust you or don't like you, don't try to extend your name or your brand.

All the above seems to sound like we are against new brands, brand extensions, and new branding partners. Not so. Innovation in products and services is the lifeblood of any organization. But, you have to sort through the babble to find sensible extensions of your current brands. Remember, the odds of breaking through with a new brand aren't good anyway—about one in five or ten—so give yourself every edge you can. Or, if you have big bucks to expend, ignore these warnings and follow the trail of the brand babblers. There are lots of them out there, waiting to take your money.

A Clear-Sighted Future

So, if none of this new brand, brand extension, brand-sharing stuff or brand research methodology works very well, how in the world do you ever develop any new business? A couple of thoughts may help.

First, there really are no new products. Almost everything that needs to be done is getting done in some way or other. So, when you start to think about a new product, ask yourself: What's it going to replace? For example, the computer is simply a replacement for the calculator, which was a replacement for the abacus, which was a replacement for sticks and stones and maybe fingers and toes.

To repeat the question: What is this new product going to replace? If you can't figure that out, most consumers won't be able to either.

Second, how clear is the name and how well does it summarize the value proposition being offered? Zima spent a ton of money trying to explain what it was or maybe what it wasn't. Gatorade had a rather simple task. If Florida football players did better on this stuff, it probably would work for you, too. This goes back to the point we made in an earlier chapter about having a product that people want, which they can understand, and can relate to their lives—and, most of all, one that can make you money. Social service is a fine institution, but it has little to do with successful brands and branding.

Third, making acquaintances is easy. Making friends is hard. Having lots of buddies or mates or pals is easy. Finding a soul mate is difficult and not everyone can do it. Think of your branding challenge more as a search for a long-time soul mate, not just a one-night fling.

New products, new brands, new markets, all are key to the success of the organization. Generally, your gut feel and your common sense are the best guides until we can better understand and research people. Or, until people can understand themselves.

Next up is how to talk to people about your brand or brands and through what media. Stay with us for that exciting topic in Chapter 11.

Notes

1. Kevin J. Clancy and Peter C. Kreig, "Surviving Innovation," *Marketing Management* , March/April 2003.

11

Media Planning and Buying

Another Dismal Science?

Over two hundred years ago, Samuel Johnson called economics the "dismal science." If he had been alive today, he probably would have said the same thing about media planning and buying. Lots of theories. Many concepts. And, most of all, lots of assumptions. Yet, in terms of brands and branding, a major topic, and essentially, an unproven and perhaps even un-founded "science."

Because the question of media investments as they relate to brands and branding is such a complex and bewildering topic for many, we've divided it into two chapters. Here we'll discuss the basic concepts of media planning and buying; i.e., the rationale behind why and how media investments are made in brands and branding. Chapter 12 takes up specific approaches to the use of media to build and maintain brands.

Glorifying Your Money

Pick up any trade publication. You'll see headline after headline, such as "Dove Flies Off with $40M" [1] Or "Astra Readies Rival to

Pfizer Blockbuster: Crestor Gets $60M Backing" [2] or "$300 Million Intel Campaign Touts Centrino Technology Intro."[3] And on and on and on. Big bucks in any league but tossed around like it was chickenfeed in the brand and branding arena.

The question is, of course, does it really take mega-spending of your dollars to build, support, or revamp a brand?

Even the most rarified of elite consulting firms apparently think so. KPMG spent an estimated $35 million to change their name to BearingPoint Inc. Deloitte Consulting "invested" approximately $70 million so people would call them Braxton. And Andersen Consulting spent an estimated $170 million to change over to Accenture.[4]

Those are big sums in any industry. But, they're especially big coming from consulting companies who supposedly know, or at least tell their clients that they know, all there is to know about branding. So, maybe it does take a giant stack of dollars to play the branding game.

Or maybe it doesn't.

The question, of course, is: What did these consulting firms get in return? It's clear for one. PricewaterhouseCoopers changed the name of its consulting unit to "Monday," sold itself to IBM, which, then, promptly scuttled the new Monday moniker, kit and caboodle.

Who profited? Obviously the brand babblers who convinced PwC to take on a name with connotations that most everybody hates. But it lasted only long enough for the new owners to bail out of it. There's clear brand thinking for you.

But, it's not just the consulting companies that spend it up on brands. Citibank was reported to have spent over $1 billion to change its name to Citi.[5] a couple of years ago. Somehow, it seems they could have cut the "bank" off their logo for less than that. Or at least gotten more back than just a shorter corporate name.

Returns, Not Spending, Are What Count

What did these corporate stalwarts get for their brand investments? Quicker recognition by clients, customers, and maybe the press?

Employee buy-in to turn in their Deloitte jackets and business cards in for ones saying Braxton? Bushels of new business pouring through the bank or consulting doors? Or did they just get a warm feeling knowing they had played the brand game and played by the rules. Spent lots of money on something only they and maybe a few others cared about? Or could even remember a few months later.

In short, the key question is: What did the firm get in return for their brand investment? We know what they spent, or said they spent, but what did they get back?

One of the major problems with marketing, advertising, and brand promotion today is: We glorify spending. We ignore returns.

Think about it.

Marketers are judged on how much they spend in "measured media" or "above and below the line marketing communication." That's the basic press story: spending. Little or no attention is given to returns, that is, whether the firm grew or went broke. (We only care about them going broke when they can't pay the agency or the media.)

Agencies are evaluated in the same way. How much in billings did they generate? How large are their accounts, always in terms of spend, never in relation to returns?

For example: A recent article in *Advertising Age* described Chrysler's mega-buck deal with Celine Dion as spokesperson as "costing [Chrysler] millions of dollars in talent fees," not to mention the huge investments the firm will also make in media time and other marketing activities. What will Chrysler get back? According to the story " . . . [the association with Celine, hopefully,] will lift the brand out of its sales doldrums," whatever that means.[6]

Glorification of spending. Minimal attention on returns. What a nutty business.

So, what does all this brand spending mean and is it really necessary?

Can't We Spend More, Boss?

Visit any marketing organization. The guy in the corner office with the green plants is quickly identifiable as the one who spends the most. The guys who don't have much to spend, although they might generate greater returns for the firm, are in a back room, steel desk and bare lightbulb hanging over their heads.

We lionize spending. We ignore returns.

It's exciting to learn a :30 commercial in the Super Bowl cost $2 million. If that is too rich for your blood, how about $1.4 million for the Academy Awards? We get excited about the "upfront" television market that runs into the billions. Yet, the TV network's share of audience continues to decline and estimated returns are plummeting as well. Is a TV schedule of commercials really worth about as much as the Gross Domestic Product of many emerging nations?

But, in the branding business, we run the spots, ignore returns and move on.

What's the next big spending opportunity? Is there an Olympics coming up? What about the Grammys, or the NBA finals, or the multitude of "media created events" designed to drain the marketer's pocketbook?

How do we rate advertisers and their importance? By how much they spend. General Motors has been one of the top measured media spenders for decades. *Advertising Age* reported that the company spent over $3,652,000,000 on measured advertising in 2002. Yet, in the first six months of that year, the company's share dipped almost 25 percent.[7]

Chevrolet, a GM brand, is one of the top spending auto name plates at over $800 million annually.[8] Does it really require that much to keep Chevrolet in the consideration set of prospective buyers? Do people really need to have "Like a rock" beaten into their heads day after day so they'll remember a tune focused on a product they will likely never buy?

Consider the plight of Kmart: Tons of money spent on advertising, both product and brand, right up to Chapter 11 time. Were they building a brand with all that spending? Consumers apparently didn't think so as they deserted the stores in droves.

As an industry, we glorify spending and we ignore returns. To paraphrase the Broadway song from Pearlie: "That's the way it is, and, that's the way it's always gonna be."

Is There Reason to All This Irrationality?

Why do brand organizations commit enormous sums to promote their brand? Bragging rights. A "Mine's bigger than yours" slap at competition. Or maybe there's no real plan at all. Maybe it's simply to "cover all the bases, not with a doily—with a blanket."

The truth is, big spending on brands and branding is likely irrational but common practice.

That brings us to the question: How much is really needed to build a brand?

That question, i.e., how much is really needed to establish a brand or reinvigorate an existing one is probably, as they say in the legal trade, unknowable. But there are some reasonable and rational things brand owners can and should know before committing to a media-based branding program that costs several years of future profits.

Instead of starting with spending, you should start with returns. How much do you want or must you get back on your branding investment? If it's 2 percent, that sets one parameter. If it's 25 percent, that's totally different.

So, drive the brand babblers nuts at the first meeting. Insist on talking about returns on your brand investment, not on how much it takes to buy time or space or change the colors or develop a "radically appealing new logo."

Remember, the branding gurus, agencies, media and their cohorts are intent on getting you to "buy," to get you to "invest" on the front-end. Not to getting you a "return" on the back end.

So, start with returns. When asked your brand budget, say: "I need a 7 percent return on this investment" or "I need this to pay out in 24 months or whatever." Then ask: "How much will it take to get this level of return leverage on my branding investment?"

Watch how fast the brand babblers start to retreat into "Brands are a long-term investment" or "We can't really measure the financial returns on brands and branding." Or, the mother of all branding responses: "Trust us, this will work. We can't prove it, but we've got a lot of experience." The experience, of course, is in buying branding stuff, not in generating financial returns from brand investments.

David Metzger

The Media Mix . . . or Mixture . . . or Conglomeration

The philosophy is simple: You spend money on brand and branding activities. You have to get money back. Always start with that concept in mind.

Granted, brands and branding are long-term investments. Returns may not come in the next 90 to 120 days, but they must occur in some reasonable time frame just like any other investment you make in your business.

You must have a brand investment financial model, pure and simple. Dollars out. Dollars back in.

Why Attitudinal Models Can't Get Financial Answers

We've harped on this before, but it's worth repeating. Attitudinal models of brand and branding returns simply can't be connected to financial returns. All the marketing "genii" have tried, for over fifty years, and no one has done it yet. And they are not likely to do it with your brand investment.

So, to look at your brand as a strategic part of your business, eschew the attitudinal models such as the Hierarchy of Effects or DAGMAR (as discussed in Chapter 4). They simply can't provide financial answers.

Unfortunately, the rub is that most of the investment models brand babblers bring to the party are focused on soft measures of returns: "mind share," or "share of voice," or "GRP levels," or even "increases in awareness," or "gains in intent to buy" and the like. Convenient terms for buying and spending—all based on a tonnage model. "Spend as much as you possibly can" or "spend more than your competitors." Or "the industry norm for spending is . . . ."

There must be a better way.

Cut through the babble. Focus on financial models of brand investments. That means you must understand financial brand returns.

Short-Term vs. Long-Term

There are two ways to think about brand investments. One is the short-term financial return you get back from your marketing and communication spending. That includes things such as the number of units you want or must sell to keep the business going, the short-term cash flows created, quarterly goals and the like. This isn't as much brand investing as it is in keeping the business healthy and growing. So, let's call these short-term investments "Business-Building." While some brand development and brand building likely occurs as a result of these short-term investments, the real goal is to generate incremental sales. So, think of these short-term investments as ways to grow the business in the short-term.

The long-term returns, or what we call "Brand-Building," take time. It is generally accomplished over years, not financial quarters. That's why these types of returns are typically difficult to measure and evaluate. Let's face it: There aren't many marketing or communication concepts or even measurement tools that are designed to evaluate long-term returns. That's why the babblers never talk about long-term measurement very much. They lack the tools, and mostly, the disciplines to measure long-term returns. So, they talk about long-term investments and let it go at that.

But, there is a way to identify and measure long-term returns on brand investments. It comes from the financial area of the business, and it is generally wrapped up in confusing topic called "brand valuation."

A brand valuation measures the current and future value of your firm's intangible brand assets in financial terms. It is rooted in the idea of ongoing income flows that customers will likely provide your company in the future through future purchases. You might think about it as the value your brand creates with customers now and into the future that encourages them to continue to do business with you and to recommend your brands to friends and associates. In short, it's really unrecognized corporate value that is created by the customer's relationship with your brand.

True, a brand's financial value is harder to measure than immediate sales, but it is just as vital to the organization for that is where your brand investments really begin to pay off.

The Babbler Challenge

One of the first things you want to do when you when you start to consider brand investments is to confront the babblers and their spending plans with this question: "Are the returns I will get back from my brand investments going to be short-term Business-Building returns—i.e. returns in the current year—or will they be longer term Brand-Building in nature, i.e., over several years?"

See what type of response you get. You can quickly tell if you're dealing with a brand babbler or a brand builder.

Brands Are About Equity

Brand valuation naturally brings up the topic of brand equity—another confusing topic that has multiple meanings. In our view, brand equity encompasses both the perceptual values attached to the brand (i.e., what people think or feel about it) as well as the financial values that result from positive customer brand behaviors (i.e., what they do that helps us make money). We make investments in branding activities in order to create positive brand associations in the minds of customers with the intention that these investments will be paid back through marketplace behaviors, primarily in the form of profitable sales. Thus, our view of brand equity includes attitudinal, behavioral, and financial aspects. It cannot be gauged without a keen understanding of all three.

Unfortunately, most babble on the subject of brand equity has been all about consumer attitudes and feelings, almost to the exclusion of the behavioral or financial aspects of brands. This has given us a very distorted view of brand equity. It's like the blind men who tried to describe an elephant from the limited perspective of the area of the animal they could touch. Most of the brand babblers see only the attitudinal aspects of equity. A limited number have begun to understand how brand equity can be measured in behaviors, such as customer loyalty, repurchase, cross purchasing, and so on. And even fewer still can speak about the most important aspect of brand equity, that is, the financial value of the brand that results from customer behaviors.

Long-term brand financial value, at least in the sense that your cash resources are invested in various types of brand activities, clearly are at the heart in this thing we call brand equity, i. e., as measured by the level of financial return your brand generates over time and the stability of that return. While it sounds complex, it really isn't.

The key, of course, is ultimately you must measure your brand equity in financial terms, not solely in attitudinal or awareness or recall terms. That can be done, but, it requires some expertise that attitudinally based babblers generally don't have. That's why they try to avoid the subject.

Today, there are several ways to estimate or calculate the financial value of a brand. All require a modicum of financial background and experience (something most brand gurus have avoided and something almost all the brand design folks don't even consider).

To get you started in understanding financial equity calculations, know that most are based on either (a) a royalty rate, that is, what a third party would pay you to use your brand in the marketplace or (b) some type of calculation or estimation of net present value or discounted cash flows. This is a matter of estimating or calculating what the income attributed to your brand (separate from the income to other tangible or intangible assets) might be in the future and then discounting it back to the present to account for the risk and the time value of money. Any accountant or financial person is familiar with the terms if not the actual calculations. But these will start you on the right track.

For the most part, these approaches will give you an idea of what your brand is worth now so you can start to measure whether it is growing or declining as you move into the future.

These base measures are important for they allow you to start building a brand scorecard or brand value tracking system. These annual or semi-annual measures allow you to determine whether your brand investments are increasing or decreasing the financial value of your brand equity over time. Those are critical measures to have for any brand financial investment and return model.

Remember, however, the key element in any type of brand valuation model is to measure the financial returns from your investments. Getting "a one percent increase in brand awareness and it only cost us $2 million" is a sure and well-worn path to the poorhouse. Kmart had incredible brand awareness when they took bankruptcy. Look what that awareness got them!

Removing the Branding Hocus-Pocus

Brand investing is really a simple matter. If you have some idea of what type of return you need or want, you can start to build or estimate some type of closed-loop investment model such as the example below.

This simple little model shows that if the firm knows the present dollar value of its customers, it can then start to make future investments in those customers over time. Direct and indirect kinds of messages to potential customers exert an influence, hopefully positive, on current customers, How positive? Measure future behavior—i.e., behavior after the messages were sent. What do you measure? Increases in spending by the customers and, thus, income to the firm. By measuring the value of those same customers in the future, a determination can be made of the return that was achieved on the initial investment. We call it a "closed-loop" approach because it is a methodology that feeds back into itself. It enables you to track the return on your brand investments over time, from initial value to future value after the investment was made.

While the model in Exhibit 6.1 is very simple, it raises some interesting questions. It suggests your brand will be bought by people

Exhibit 11.1

CLOSED-LOOP SYSTEMS

Measurable, Marketer-Controlled Brand Messages

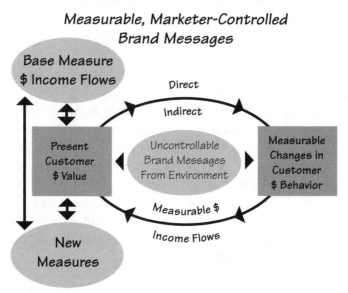

or customers, not by market segments or demographic age groups. That's why the boxes say "Customer," not "target markets" or "geographic segments" or some other clever marketing term. Your investments in brand communication of any type have to do with trying to influence people to get them to do something on behalf of your brand, specifically, to plunk down their hard cash to buy *your* branded product or service, not your competitors'.

To repeat, it is consumer or customer behaviors that count in brands and branding, not just good feelings or recognition or even people wearing your Tee shirts. It is only logical to assume that people will only spend their money on your brand after they have those good feelings, but the good feelings, like good intentions, alone are not enough. If positive behavior doesn't follow, those good feelings are worthless. Branding is, or should be, a commercial venture, not a test to see who can spend the most or develop the most good feelings or "creative" messages.

A lot of the babble about branding has to do with media, media investments, media buying and media exposure. While some of these concepts and approaches may have some value to you, not all are important. In the next chapter, we'll cut through the media babble that compounds and confuses the challenge of managing your brand. Especially in determining how much or, better said, how little you can or should invest in your brand.

Notes

1. "Doves Flies off with $40M" *Brandweek*, July 14, 2003, p. 14.
2. "Astra Readies Rival to Pfizer Blockbuster: Crestor Gets $60M Backing," *Advertising Age*, July 21, 2003, p. 1.
3. *Brandweek*, March 3, 2003, p. 5.
4. *BtoB Magazine*, Nov 11, 2002.
5. Tim Teran, "From Global to Icon: Tales of Evolution at Citi," Presentation at Marketing Science Institute, Milan, Italy, June 20–21, 2000.
6. "The Gospel of Peter: Arnell on A Mission," *Advertising Age*, Nov. 18, 2002.
7. "Age Leading Advertisers," *Advertising Age*, July 17, 2003.
8. *Advertising Age*, July 24, 2002.

12

Why Branding Doesn't Take a Ton of Media Spending

Some of the worst brand babbling of the new millennium comes from all the old-line, old-time brand-building baggage that survived the turn of the century. Mass media, mass markets, mass communication, i.e., mass any-and-everything, still sits on the brand-building station platform as part and parcel of the "branding train." The problem, however, is that old concept of brands and branding left the station years ago and likely won't return.

Mass marketing, while it still makes sense in developing countries, has less and less to do with building and maintaining successful brands in established markets, i.e., North America, Europe, Japan, Australia, etc. This is not to say that mass communication is not helpful for brand-building, but it does say it is not the only approach, as many of the babblers, particularly in the agencies and media, would want you to believe.

Earlier, we discussed why the "Industrial Age" concepts, practices, and mentality that built brands fifty years ago are simply inappropriate for today's global, interconnected, networked, mobile economies, customers, and consumers. We explore the babbling about media advertising in this chapter.

History Isn't Always Our Friend

For the brand babblers, historical success is always used as a reference. No doubt, mass advertising built brands in the 1950s and influenced the development and use of brands up to the late 1980s. Those successes are hard to forget, particularly when the principles and concepts that created those "mega-brands" are still being hawked by the trade press, advertising agencies, media organizations, brand consultants, and the like. But, you must remember, all of these "brand hawkers" have a vested interest in seeing those worn-out principles and concepts maintained. Yet, if your goal is to develop programs that will generate returns on your brand investments in the twenty-first century, many of the historical examples you see and hear referenced are and will not be terribly relevant in today's marketplace.

Rut-Bound Media Thinking

Much of the difficulty of moving forward is the current media thinking that's stuck in the mass media morass. The media planning and buying models used today have been codified and verified and lionized to the point that no one even questions them anymore. For example, terms such as reach, frequency, coverage, duplication, and audience accumulation are tossed around willy-nilly. Few, if any, people bother to look under the hood and see what those terms mean or meant and even if they are relevant today. We just "buy into them" and move on. Generally to the detriment of our branding ROI.

For example, the concept of frequency of three as the ideal number of advertising exposure, is based on a hypothesis developed in 1965. Although widely accepted, it has never been proven in the marketplace. Yet, every media model existent uses this 3X approach with no real basis or reason for being. It's just part of the lore of historical branding. Look at any media plan. What do you see: attempts to reach the magic "three." Why? Just because it has become a media maxim.

That's right. Most of our media planning concepts are holdovers from a bygone era. They assume audiences are made up of families similar to "Ozzie and Harriett and the boys" sitting in front of a scratchy-image, 17-inch B&W television set, breathlessly waiting for the next episode of "Gunsmoke" . . . and, your brand's :60 commercial. It just ain't like that anymore.

So, when the media babblers come knocking with their statistics-filled overheads, asking for big bucks to support a "brand-building campaign," ask them to explain a few simple concepts:

- What's the basis for the frequency of three in media planning? (Note: don't let them shift into Effective Frequency. That has the same problems.)
- How can unduplicated audiences exist in today's media pervasive, interactive marketplace?
- Is there really any such thing as "media continuity" when audiences ebb and flow on an almost minute-by-minute basis?

And, if you really want to throw down the gauntlet, ask: "Network television ratings and viewerships are going down. Prices are going up. Is television really the best way to build a brand today? And, if you think so, why?"

The answers you'll get commonly won't be very satisfactory because there aren't many good answers. That's because those questions have to do with generating returns from media expenditures, not from buying more media. You're asking for what you'll get back. The media folks are focused on what you send out and on how many dollars you put behind your "media campaign."

The challenge of media buying is simple: "Outputs" in terms of messages or "stuff sent out" versus "outcomes" or "returns on the sending of those things." The problem is, you'll very seldom hear about outcomes. Media planning and buying is all about "outputs." Brand owners and managers should be focused on "outcomes." Outcomes are money coming back into the firm, not money going out. Hopefully, some day, the twain will meet. But they haven't so far.

Selling Unknowns

Media people don't really know how many people will actually see your brand message. Everything they do is based on "estimated audiences," and the primary measure is "opportunities to see or hear," not those who actually did see or hear. So, we don't really know if anyone saw our advertising. All we really know is that we sent it out.

Just because your brand guru or agency can't give you answers, don't think the media owners can do any better. They can't. All they know is that they created the "opportunity to see or hear"; i.e., "We sent the magazine out. We don't know if anyone looked at it." Or, "We broadcast the radio commercial. We don't really know if anyone heard it." So, you're really buying estimates, not audiences. Potential eyes and ears, not real eyes and ears.

And that was fine in the 1950s. Statistical analysis in terms of sampling and projections were pretty solid then. Few media. Interested audiences. Limited commercialization. Remember when we used to broadcast :60 commercials? Now they're often :10s or :15s at the most. The same old tune in advertising: Pay more, get less.

A few years ago, there was a television media concept called "road-blocking," which meant that you bought a commercial on all three networks at the same time. People watching television couldn't miss your message—and they couldn't see your competitors' because you had taken all the available space. Try that today, when many homes receive 150 to 200 channels. See the problem? The media landscape has changed. Media planning and buying hasn't. And, media buying and planning to build and manage brands is about the same as it was in 1970. Is your product or service or your customer the same as it was 35 years ago?

So, before you plunk down mega-bucks to buy a media schedule to "build your brand with your target audience," remember: All you're really buying is the *opportunity* for someone to see or hear. No guarantee they are there. Set may be on. Person may be out.

The key ingredient in reviewing a media plan for your brand introduction, or brand maintenance, or brand re-positioning, or whatever is that media is focused on "outputs" while what you need are "outcomes," i.e., people demanding your brand or buying it in place of a competitor. Unfortunately, media people can't do that even though they project their "estimates" to the fourth decimal place.

What's Really Challenging Media Buying Today

Having railed against present-day media planning and buying systems, what proof is there that these time-honored systems are obsolete?

Easy. Look around you. What do you see? People multi-tasking. For example, people using multiple media systems all at the same time. It's called simultaneous media exposure, and it is rampant around the world. This is one of the major challenges of media in this decade, yet, it is the one that continues to be ignored.

What happened? For one, the media spectrum is vastly different than it was in the 1960s. More media forms. More pervasive. More continuous.

Media consumers are different, too. They live in an interactive, networked, mobile, "sound-bite" world of telephones, computers, DVD players, Sony Walkmen, and, yes, newspapers and magazines and over-the-air television.

Today, the consumer's exposure to media is through multiple systems and channels and it is simultaneous and almost continuous. They're on line, watching TV, and looking at a magazine, all at the same time. They're reading the newspaper, listening to the radio, and talking on the mobile telephone . . . all at the same time. It's quite clearly simultaneous media usage.

Some Simultaneous Evidence

In a research study conducted fall, 2002, in the US, Schultz and Pilotta found over 50 percent of the study's respondents reported they were multi-tasking with various forms of media during the prime evening 7 to 11 p.m. time period.[1] One chart from that study is shown below.

So much for focused, unduplicated media exposures to interested and involved audiences. That's what you're getting with your media dollar, but it's not what you think you are buying.

So, media has changed. Consumers have changed. Media planning and media buying have not. That's the problem. And it explains why brand babblers recommend investing inordinate amounts of money to support brands. They're all supportive of "tonnage media

Exhibit 12.1

PRIME TIME MEDIA USAGE

135% of the population use some combination of TV, Online, and Magazines simultaneously

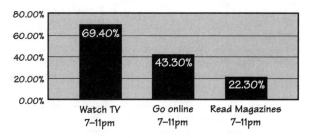

models." To win at the tonnage game, you have to increase your brand spend often to unheard of amounts. In other words, to compensate for changed media facilities, media habits and changed consumers, the babblers do what they do best, i.e., buy more, spend more, hope more.

Quick, Give Me an Answer

Hopefully we've shaken your faith in the $230 billion US media planning and buying market. But what do we recommend? Are increasing the number of messages or the frequency or the noise level, all of which cost more, the only way to deliver your brand messages or incentives?

One answer: Flip the media planning and buying process upside-down. Move from an outbound only, media-focused spending approach to one focused on brand contacts or brand touchpoints.

Rather than starting with the media that you might purchase, start at the other end of the pipe, that is, people who are already touching you, your company, your brand in some way or another. They have reached out to you. What message or incentive are they receiving from that brand "touchpoint?" What are those "touchpoints" saying to customers and prospects about your brand and your brand experience? So, media planning in the twenty-first century should start with how customers and consumers are coming in contact with your brand, not what media plans you are developing or what media programs you might buy. Start with customers and work backward.

Exhibit 12.2

PLANNING BRAND CONTACTS

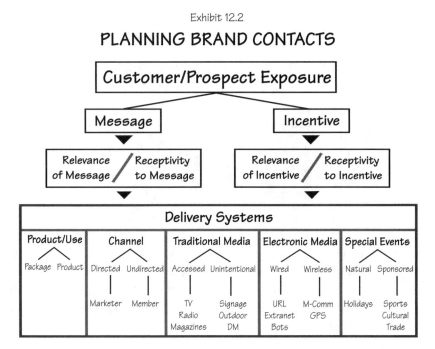

Identify how or when or where the people who might be your best brand customers or prospects might or do come in contact with you, your brand, your company, or your value proposition. Try to be there, when they are there. It's that simple, although it's not that easy. But, then, if you're looking for something easy, just add a few million more to your mass media spend.

Touchpoints, Not Media Systems

What this requires, of course, is knowing something about customers and prospects. Not about media audiences. Who your customers are. Who the best prospects are. Where and when they come in contact with you and your brand. But, remember, that's what branding is all about: building and maintaining relationships. If you don't know who you want to build a relationship with, how can messages thrown out in the mass media help?

Once you learn who your best customers and prospects are and how they come in contact with you, take the next step. Try to determine which of those contacts are most relevant and meaningful to customers and prospects and when they would like to hear from you. Not when you would like to talk—when they would like to listen.

Exhibit 12.2 is a simple little chart that helps you think about brand contacts in a different way.

An example will help. Assume you're in the coffee business. Your goal is to retain your present customers and at the same time get them to try your new flavored coffee line. The traditional way would be to develop a nifty commercial with people singing and dancing to a swell new tune about your flavored coffee. Buy some television time targeted to women 34+. Throw out a few coupons and see what happens.

The alternative is to start at the other end of the system. You have a group of loyal and dedicated customers. Some of them would likely be interested in trying your new flavored coffee product. So, start to think about where they come in contact with your brand now. Obviously in or on the package is one way. Maybe a trial coupon inserted in the package. Where else do they see or come in contact with you. At the supermarket shelf. Maybe a few shelf-talkers or "flashing red arrows" to call attention to your new product. They obviously are more interested in coffee when appropriate times come in their own lives. People use coffee in the morning. Maybe a coupon delivered to homes in the morning newspaper would be best. Or, perhaps some trial programs for social clubs or maybe a home page on coffee with history, background, and how your new product was developed would get attention. In short, start with customers and prospects and work back. Don't just start with what media you can buy or what promotions you can run that might attract attention. Start with brand contacts, where customers and prospects come in contact with you.

As is clear from the model in the chart above, all we have done is toss the basic concepts of outbound media planning and buying out the window. The focus is not how you want to talk to customers and prospects; it's how they want to hear from you. Not in the media forms you want to buy; in the media forms they already rely on and use. When you flip the process upside-down, you open up a multitude of alternative ways to reach or touch customers and prospects with brand messages. And only a few of them involve the traditional media planning and buying concepts you're using now.

Clearly, the "touch-points" approach is just the opposite of how most brand babblers attack the problem. That's why it's usually so much more effective and so much less expensive.

David Metzger

The Media-by-the-Ton Method

A Word from the Third Parties

Today, it is all the rage to hear branding mavens suggest the real way to build brands is through public relations or third-party endorsements. There's nothing wrong with that. One of our good friends and colleagues at Northwestern University, Tom Harris, invented the concept, term, and practice called "Marketing Public Relations." But, Tom will be the first to tell you: Brands aren't built solely with public relations any more than they're built solely with advertising. Indeed, the real work of brand building is done through integrated marketing communications approaches, not through massive programs of *only* advertising or *only* promotion or *only* PR. Remember, the bucks you are spending are yours. At some point they will run out if you don't do the branding thing right.

Integrated marketing communications or IMC is the concept of first developing a sound, consistent, customer-focused brand strategy and then implementing that strategy with consistent, coordinated, customer-focused marketing communications activities. Not just advertising. Not just PR. Not just interactive or on line. A total, complete approach to building relationships with customers and prospects across all possible points of relevant brand contact.

So, the next time one of those high-priced, smooth-talking brand "experts" says "Build your brand with advertising" or "Build your brand with public relations" or "Build your brand with viral or permission or guerilla or interactive or experiential marketing or communication . . . " tell them to "back off." You're not going to drink the single-medium Kool-Aid. You know it takes an integrated approach to build a brand.

In summary, you probably shouldn't rely on a single medium to build a brand and you definitely don't need to spend a ton of money on media to build a brand either. Dell Computers didn't. Starbucks didn't. Wal-Mart didn't. They seem to have figured out how to build a brand using all the touch points they have with customers, not just relying on massive media advertising investments. With a little thought, you should be able to do that, too.

The Proof Is Getting Money Back, Not Spending Your Way to the Poor House

The problem this new approach to building a brand creates is that, with limited media expenditures, how are you going to tell if it's working? Without being able to track media placements and media expenditures, how will you know if your "brand plan" is creating the results you want?

That's in the next chapter.

Notes

1. Paper presented at the Advertising Research Foundation, "Marketing and Media Effectiveness" Workshop, October 10, 2002.

13

Brand Tracking in the Himalayas

Nice to Know, But Not Very Useful as a Brand Measure

 $\boxed{a}$ t the other end of the spectrum from brand research (remember, Chapter 4) is brand tracking or brand measurement, i.e., what the marketer gets or got back from his or her branding investments or expenditures.

This is where the babble soars to the mountaintops!

Brand tracking in the Himalayas is facetiously used as this chapter's title. Why? Because many of today's brand measurement systems are about as useful as the searches for the Abominable Snowman, the elusive "half-man, half-animal thing" that pops up in the news now and again. Interesting at the time, but with little long-term value.

Our brand measurement discussion begins in this chapter and, because it is so important, carries over to Chapter 14.

Let's start with the granddaddy of all brand measurement: brand-tracking studies.

Follow the Bouncing Dots

Brand tracking is the most basic of all brand measurement methodologies. Simply described, it is generally based on some type of survey research that tracks people's awareness, feelings and knowledge about the brand and its messages over time. Using questions, such as, "Have you seen or heard of XYZ brand?" the goal is to determine top-of-mind awareness, that is, the brand that most people can remember first.

Assuming a positive response to earlier questions, the researcher then drills down into knowledge, preference, and so on. (Remember the Hierarchy of Effects model in Chapter 4. It's the same base for tracking studies.) The premise, of course, is that the ability to remember or recall the brand somehow or other leads to purchase, a most tenuous relationship.

Often questions about the brand's advertising are asked; e.g., Were there celebrities or animals or beautiful food shots or whatever the marketer thinks the brand message was supposed to deliver and what people ought to remember? Why? Because there is still a belief that memorability and recall of brand impressions somehow impact brand behaviors. (See how the string of logic is building?)

Those questions are followed by things such as "Do you buy or use Brand XYZ?" or maybe "Do you intend to buy Brand XYZ the next time you buy a product in that category?" (Inferential leaps from recall to purchase intent with little more than supposition to support it. Recall our discussions of brand research in Chapter 4).

The responses to all these questions are recorded, perhaps summarized, and then plotted on a graph with changes noted over time. This "brand tracking" measure supposedly tells the marketer how well his or her brand is doing in the market. Thus, the marketer can "track" the brand over time in terms of awareness, knowledge, preference, and so on (the Hierarchy of Effects revisited in some detail).

Misnomers as a Starting Place

What's really happening, though, is that this approach is really communication tracking, not brand tracking. Brand tracking would logically be related to sales or customer take-away or customer value

David Metzger

"You will meet a tall, mysterious and profitable brand . . ."

in some way. But, in most models presently in use by the babblers, it isn't. The weakness, of course, is that this type of research is not designed to include information on brand relationships, brand purchases, brand advocacy, or the like. Just memory and recall: Do people recognize the name or logo? Did they retain something of the messaging? Memory tests such as these are rampant in the marketplace today. Babblers encourage them because they are often related to brand expenditures. Not happy with your tracking scores? Probably need to spend more on media or promotion, is the general theme line.

Commonly, such methodologies contain precious little (or nothing) on the value of the brand to the customer, their loyalty or commitment to it, brand advocacy or any long-term financially based commitments that can be projected into the future.

The question "What do you, the customer or prospect, remember about my brand communication?" is the yardstick. In these measures, something is always better than nothing or so the babblers would have you believe.

But, the problem is: How much memory do you want to buy, and is memory worth anything going forward? There's not much evidence that either one is of much use.

Looking Back Over Your Shoulder to See Where You're Going

Don't get us wrong. The many marketing organizations using this type of tracking measurement have the right idea. That is, they conduct these studies annually or quarterly or even monthly in an effort to measure changes in brand memory over time. The problem, of course, is that the measures are historical; i.e., what happened in the past, not what's likely to happen in the future.

And the studies don't tell them much about the brand; they tell them about the brand messaging or brand communication. The assumption, of course, is that if you remember the jingle for my brand or my brand's logo or the celebrity I am currently promoting, you will buy and use my product or service. But, there is precious little evidence that these "connections" result in any meaningful financial impact for the organization.

The biggest value of brand tracking studies? They give brand managers and the babblers a feeling they are "doing something about brand measurement." But, not much else.

Shelf Fillers, Not Knowledge

The bigger problem of course is that brand-tracking studies cost big bucks, and, unfortunately, most brand managers don't do much with the data. Why? Because there isn't much you can do with the plotted dots except use them as an "early warning" system of poor creative, bad media buying or the like.

The time period in which the brand communication activity appeared is over. You can't do anything about that. The measures may tell you whether or not your messages are getting through. That has some value. But, if you ask the respondents where they saw the brand messages, they invariably say "on TV" (because that's where they most expect to see brand communication) even if you didn't have a television schedule. So, that makes interpretation—and, thus, practical use—not just tricky but downright conjectural.

Of course, if the brand tracking tells you that no one even knows your brand is in the marketplace or that you're investing dollars to promote it and none of your messages are getting through, you at least know you have a failure on your hands. Hopefully, you might have time to cancel any future programs until you fix this one. So tracking brand communication has value as a "disaster alert." But, you can't make much money on programs after the horse has left the barn.

Generally, though, the babblers gloss over the poor results because they reflect badly on their skills, abilities, and the fees you are paying them to guide you. So, the tracking is explained away; i.e., this is an "interim measure" or "these kinds of programs always start slowly" or "trust us, this is working, it's just too early." All of which say you've spent your money. Not much has happened. But, maybe if you spend more, things will turn up. Not a good place to be if those were your dollars that went down the drain.

So, if brand tracking studies don't tell the manager or owner much, don't really relate to future financial returns and are often explained away by the babblers, why do marketing organizations continue to do "brand tracking studies"? A true story will illustrate the level of brand measurement acuity in one supposedly sophisticated marketing organization we worked with recently.

"What We Do With Brand Tracking"

About two years ago, we got a call from a major financial services advertiser. They had just gotten notice of a substantial cost increase from their brand tracking supplier for the following year. Senior management, when presented with the cost increase, asked the marketing and marketing research people three questions prior to approval:

1. Is this tracking study worth what we pay for it?
2. What are we doing with the results?
3. Can knowing what the brand tracking system provides be used to make any measurable difference in our brand's success as a result of having the information?"

Seemingly reasonable questions from the CFO and board.

The marketer called our consulting company. "Let's talk about brand measurement . . . " was the way the opening question was framed. We asked what they were doing. That's when the brand tracking questions came up. To understand their situation, we asked some rather simple questions:

Question: "What do you do with the tracking results?"

Answer: "We show it to the board."

Question: "What does the board do with the results?"

Answer: "They look at it. If it's about the same as last period, they thank us and put it away."

Question: "So, it's disaster protection. Right?"

Answer: "No, not really. Even if our tracking results go down, they never say anything and we never do anything different."

Question: "So what do you do with the tracking reports?"

Answer: "We put them in the tracking binder and bring it out next month as an update."

Question: "So, you don't do much with it. It costs a lot. And, you don't really use it to manage the business. Is that about it?"

Answer: That's about it."

Our recommendation: "Cancel the tracking."

Response: "Oh, we couldn't do that. We'd have a break in our historical records. We'd lose continuity. It would disrupt our historical trend lines."

You can guess the rest. The organization renewed their tracking service at the higher cost. Why? Because they had always done tracking. Really no other reason. A crutch for the marketing and research folks. That's about all.

While this story might sound unique and the marketing organization a bit anal, unfortunately that's why many tracking studies continue to be done: "Because we've always done them."

Brand tracking studies do have some value if properly used. They tell you what your brand communication is doing. If you start getting answers you don't want to hear, tracking serves as an early warning. But, if you're trying to determine the value of your brand or to measure the financial impact of your brand program, or trying to determine the return on your branding investments, tracking doesn't help much. No matter what the brand babblers and the tracking promoters say.

So, if brand tracking isn't too useful, what else is out there?

Branding's Bermuda Triangle

If brand tracking is of such limited value, why not come up with something better? There have been some efforts. But, unfortunately, those haven't been too successful either. The reason is simple. They've been mostly derived from the attitudinal measures that came out of advertising communication studies. In other words, they're generally based on psychological and attitudinal measurement approaches the advertising folks invented in the 1960s, i.e., the Hierarchy of Effects, DAGMAR and the like. You already know the problems with those types of methodologies.

The big challenge? Researchers have been singularly unsuccessful in connecting attitudinal studies or even attitudinal change to any type of behavioral change. And, it's behavioral change that puts change in your pocket. You spend money on brands and branding. You must get financial returns back.

Summary: To get to financial returns, you need consumer behaviors, not just consumer attitudes. It's that simple and it's that clear. Behaviors, not just attitudes.

And, therein lies the problem.

Where the communication people have adopted the Hierarchy of Effects model, the brand babblers have gone several steps further. They've built brand models loosely based on another psychological model. This one is Maslow's "Hierarchy of Human Needs" discussed in Chapter 4. Maslow visualized his concept as a triangle with "Self-Actualization" at the top. That's where the human is motivated by the need to seek self-fulfillment and to achieve their full intellectual potential.

Maslow's premise was that as needs on one level are satisfied, humans continuously try to move up his hypothesized hierarchy. Thus, their motivations and behaviors predictably change from one level to the next. Of course, not all individuals reach the highest level in the hierarchy. Some individuals get stuck on certain levels because of economic situations, the inability to intellectualize the next level, and the like. Therefore, relatively few ever reach the top. Guess what the brand babblers have done? That's right: they've hypothesized similar models, i.e., "needs-based" approaches, to formulate brand strategies. Thus, you'll be exposed to all types of brand triangles, pyramids, and other such geometric shapes, many of them suggesting your brand can be thought of in relation to human needs; e.g., your brand can help customers solve their practical, emotional or psychological needs. In one such well-known "Brand Pyramid" functional brand benefits are depicted at the bottom, emotional benefits in the middle, and somewhere near the top, psychic and self-expressive benefits. There is nothing wrong with understanding customer motivations and trying to link your brand to deeply-felt customer needs and wants. In fact, it's an imperative of sound branding, i.e., start with rich customer insights. And, graphical representations can be a useful tool in conceptualizing complicated ideas. The danger, however, lies in using geometry as a means to oversimplify and trivialize complex issues about customers and their behavior. Too often, these tools—especially in the wrong hands—lead to shallow and formulaic conclusions about customers, and, in turn, result in superficial and ineffectual brand efforts. Like the infamous Bermuda Triangle, your money goes into them and is never seen again.

Now, when you see some type of brand triangle, you'll at least know where it came from . . . Maslow and his Hierarchy of Needs, circa the 1940s. The babblers won't tell you that. Sometimes, they don't even know the source of their hypotheses. But, we do. And, we have.

Maslovian Value

As mentioned above, the Maslow-derived triangle sometimes is a good way to think about customers and consumers and how your brand might help them meet their needs. It also might be helpful in thinking about how your various brand elements and messages need to fit together. But, don't think of these babbler-created triangles as the magic symbol that can create instant brand success. They're only a tool, and they only help you think about how customers and consumers might react to your brand. So, triangles are good, but they're not the solution to measuring the return on your brand investments.

But, wait! There's more.

If the Maslow Hierarchy works for planning, why wouldn't it work for measurement? So, you'll see many brand attitudinal measurement techniques based on the triangle or some type of needs hierarchy. Similar to the Hierarchy of Effects, the measures attempt to track changes in consumer attitudes toward the brand, generally over time. And, time is the most important ingredient if you decide to take up the Maslow-based methodologies. Only by following consumer or customer movements can you make any sense of the approach.

But, most "brand triangle" babble-figures suffer from the same challenges as advertising attitudinal models. That is an ongoing and apparently unsolvable challenge of connecting attitudes or attitudinal change to any type of financial measures. So, while the Maslow-type measurement models are sometimes revealing in terms of how people think about and what they believe about your brand, to really measure the financial value your brand is creating, you must incorporate behavioral data; e.g., what people did, not how people thought or think or imagine or dream or even how much they like your brand or even if they have "topped-out" in self-actualization. The only solution to finding out if you got something back from the bucks you spent on branding activities must include behavioral data.

Behaviors Used to be Hard, Now They're Easy

The reason we have brand measurement systems based on attitudes is clearly historical. In the 1960s, when the Hierarchy of Effects model was developed and when consumer behavior researchers first started quoting Maslow, few organizations could obtain actual behavioral data on consumers. Or, if they could, the analytical tasks were so overwhelming managers simply abandoned the attempt. Thus, attitudinal models were accepted, grew, and were formalized in the marketing and communication literature simply because they could be done and they provided a better solution than no solution at all. And, statistically, we could take small samples of the population and project them to the whole, if we assumed our customers were distributed on a "normal curve." In the last ten years, however, technology has made behavioral data so easy to obtain through various forms, such as loyalty programs, purchase records and the like, that many marketing organizations are literally swimming in data. Thus, the major problem is not getting behavioral data; it's figuring out what to do with the data once you have it.

Having behavioral data enables the brand marketer to know what customers and prospects did as a result of their marketing and communication efforts. That is, they can directly tie marketing communication efforts to changes in behaviors. For example: "We ran a brand communication program." "Did some people become a customer as a result?" "Did present customers buy more or buy more often?" "Did competitive users switch from their brand to ours?" "Did customers reduce their purchases of competitive products?" And so on through some relevant process of learning.

The beauty of behavioral data, of course, is that it enables marketers to determine, financially, what customers did as a result of their brand marketing and communication investments. Today, marketers can truly start to develop models and processes that say "This many dollars were spent on brand marketing" and "This many dollars came back from the customers who received that brand communication." Remember our "closed-loop model" from Chapter 11? This makes it possible.

Today, it's behavioral data that makes measurement of brand investments and evaluation of brand programs possible. Of course, behavioral data really challenges the babblers psychological models and they don't like that. So, they rant and rail and continue to try and sell you, the brand owner, a package of out-of-date awareness and attitudinal measures that they dress up in new and exciting lingo to disguise the basic weaknesses of the approaches.

So, a caution: Beware the brand babbler with triangles and flow charts of "needs-based" measures. Most of the need is on their end, not yours and, in most cases, not on your customers and prospects either.

The availability and use of behavioral data signals a major change in how brand value and returns on your brand investments can and should be measured. That's one of the key concepts you should take from this book.

Does the growth of behavioral data mean attitudinal data is worthless or useless? No. It simply means that attitudinal data should be used to explain the observed consumer behaviors, rather than trying to predict future consumer behaviors from attitudinal change.

The difference in the uses of attitudinal and behavioral data to measure and evaluate brands is critical to brand success. That's the next chapter.

14

Searching For Brand Equity in All the Right Places

in the previous chapter, we argued that customer behavioral data could be used to identify and determine the returns that came from our brand investments. That's important because quantifying brand returns gives us a better grip on understanding the brand's financial value, a term used intermittently in the last few chapters

In this chapter we focus on the financial dimensions of brand value—that is, the estimation or valuation of the brand's financial worth to the brand owner.

But first, we must examine another branding term around which much babbling exists: brand equity. Obviously, *brand equity* has been borrowed from the financial arena. So it must have something to do with money. Right? Maybe, but maybe not.

Also, the term *equity* implies some type of ownership. It includes the ideas and perceptions that both customers and consumers "own" about the brand as well as the rights of ownership enjoyed by the company that bears legal title to the name, symbols, and other attributes of the brand.

A third point is that brand equity can change over time—either increasing or decreasing as a result of changing customer attitudes, loyalties, behaviors, and market performance. These all have a direct impact on the increase or decrease of the brand's economic value to its owner.

The brand's financial value, as we discuss it in this chapter, is related to, but not the same as, its brand equity. We will use brand equity as a more generalized term reflecting the brand as a marketing asset. As our colleague at the London School of Business, Tim Ambler, explains: The value of the asset is separate from the nature of the asset itself; i.e., your house and the price you can get for it are not the same thing. You can live in your house but not in a pile of dollar bills. While we are all familiar with understanding how financial equity is built up in our homes, we are far less knowledge about understanding how the financial value of our brands is built and monitored over time.

The Elusive Brand Equity Yardstick

If you define brand equity as the value customers place on your brand (as Kevin Lane Keller, David Aaker, Roland Rust, and others have done), you would measure the strength of the relationship consumers or end-users have with your brand. Those measures would likely include things such as brand satisfaction, perceptions about the brand, preference of your brand to competitors, willingness to pay a price premium, brand advocacy, and several other consumer-based, measures. This would reflect the brand equity in the minds of customers and prospects. A very useful concept.

But, as we have said earlier, the brand creates value for both customers as well as for the organizations that own them. So, at the other end of the yardstick are the financial measures relating to the economic worth of the brand. As discussed in an earlier chapter, the brand, from the brand owner's view, is an intangible asset that has financial value. For example, you, as the brand owner, if you wanted to, could sell your brand to another organization, for example, the way Philip Morris sold Miller beer to South African Breweries. If only the brand, and not some of the tangible resources used to produce, distribute or market it, was sold, the value would be the brand value. In other words, the financial value of the brand is the price paid above the dollar value of the tangible, fixed assets

David Metzger

The Measurement Challenge:
Making Sure All the Right Pieces are in the Right Places

associated with the brand, less any other identifiable intangible assets, such as copyrights, patents, and so on. In this view, the buyer and seller would agree on the selling price and thus, inherently agree on the brand value being either sold or purchased. So far, so good.

There are ways to measure a brand's financial value. The surest, of course, is our example above, i.e., what some person or company would pay you, the owner, for the brand, cash on the barrelhead.

But, most organizations can't or don't make money buying and selling brands. They make money by owning brands and receiving the current and future income streams from them. If you get greater income from the brand than your investment in operating the brand, you have positive cash flows and therefore the financial value of the brand will increase. And that's what shareholders and owners like.

So, the basic economic premise of brand communication is that you invest in brand communication programs today in the hope of influencing what consumers do in the future because that will create future financial value for you, the brand owner. There is ample evidence that those future brand flows come from changes or reinforcement of consumers' and customers' behaviors, not just because they change their attitudes. Typically, those behavioral changes result in future income flows over time, but they may create negotiating value if you decide to sell now.

Thus, from the brand owner's perspective, the brand's financial value is all about investing dollars in or on behalf of the brand now and receiving greater dollars back in the future. Tim Ambler, has referred to this as "unrealized financial gains" for the organization.[1]

So, a simple definition of the brand's financial value is just that; the realistic expectation of getting more money back in the future than you have already invested today. One might think of it as a financial reservoir that the brand owner might draw upon over time or the returns the owner will enjoy in the future as a result of actions today.

Customer Income Flows Are Key

In the simplest and most depersonalized terms, customers are nothing more than a series of income flows for the organization now and into the future. Thus, brand management is really a case of managing customer income flows and assuring their continuation.

Most brand managers don't see it that way, of course. They see the brand as a product or service with channels of distribution, pricing, and all the other marketing paraphernalia that go with being in the marketplace. In short, all that marketing lingo they learned in their MBA courses. But, deep down, when you pluck all the feathers, the brand is nothing more than an ongoing relationship in which a customer exchanges financial value with the marketing organization for the use of the benefits the brand provides.

That's why customer behaviors are so much more critical in understanding brand value than attitudinal measures are. If customers don't behave by purchasing the product or service, no income flow is created no matter how positive their attitudes or thoughts might be.

If brands are really surrogates for customer income flows, then managing the brand means managing the customer income flows. So, successful brands have lots of customers with lots of income flows. Unsuccessful brands have fewer customers and, therefore, fewer or smaller income flows.

If you, as the brand owner, don't spend all the income flows the customer provides, you make a profit, and that's what most organizations are trying to do with their brands: make a profit.

Understanding the Drivers of the Brand's Financial Value

Understanding the financial aspects of the brand rests on four key elements:

1. The number of customers the brand has and the income flows they create over time. Obviously, the more customers, the greater the income flows. This is a basic, traditional measure used in estimating future cash flows.
2. The brand's ability to attract new customers. Clearly, the brand is going to need new customers as old ones leave, die, change to competitors or change their lifestyles, making the brand no longer appropriate. Brands that continuously gain new customers faster than they lose the old ones are healthy brands.
3. The brand's contribution to margins, that is, the excess in income flows over the costs associated in providing the brand to the customer above and beyond those that can be attributed to the firm's tangible assets alone. If the brand has many customers who truly value the brand over the competition, are willing to pay a premium price, or use the brand more often, then the brand will have a significant, measurable impact on operating margins.
4. The stability of the customer income flows to the firm over time. This relates to the continuing loyalty of customers who purchase. Thus, the overall income flows to the brand owner must be leveled out over time.

When one examines these elements, an estimate of the brand's value can be obtained. The brand's financial value can be seen as the residual value the firm can create in the future as a result of (a) the total number of customers the brand has, (b) the brand's ability to attract additional customers, (c) the brand's contribution to operating margins, and (d) the stability of the income flows generated by customers. And, all of this is then projected into the future, commonly three to five years out.

So, understanding the financial dimensions of brand value is that simple and certainly not as complex as the Babblers would have you believe.

Simplifying the Complex

The brand owner must know three things to be able to determine how successful the brand is and to be able to define the value that the brand marketing and communication program has created:

1. Is the program generating more customers for the brand so that income flows will increase?
2. Is the program increasing the margins the brand can generate from its customers over time?
3. Does the brand communication help assure you, as the brand owner, of continuing income flows into the future by building relationships with customers so that they continue to buy your brand over time? Are those income flows stable or one-time occurrences?

While the questions seem simple, the answers, or, at least the methodologies to generate those answers, quickly become quite complex. And that's where the babbling really goes over the edge . . . and top. And, if you're not watchful, it will take you and your brand with it.

Complex Measures to Get to Simple Answers

Today, there are two basic ways to determine the financial value of your brand. First is the so-called "royalty rate." This measure shows, generally in terms of some type of percentage of sales or levy per unit, what you would have to pay the brand owner to use the brand in the marketplace. In other words, it would be the royalty rate or franchise fee or other payment you would pay the brand owner to use the brand to generate the income flows from your customers who are buying the brand you have acquired for marketplace use.

The second type of brand valuation measure is some type of discounted cash flow calculation or net present value estimate based on forward-looking estimates of sales and profits. This type of financial calculation tells the brand owner what the future value of his or her customer brand income flows would be worth over some period of time. It's based on the simple financial principle that money today is worth more than money tomorrow. Thus, customer income flows today are worth more than customer income flows in the future. In other words, if you, as the brand owner, invest a dollar in the brand today, what would the resulting income flow from the customers who responded to that dollar investment be worth in the future, i.e., three, five, seven, or more years from now. This is a fairly standard accounting calculation that has substantial acceptance in all financial circles.

The goal of brand communication is, of course, to invest current dollars in the brand today through various forms of brand communication. The expectation would be that the future income flows would be worth more over time, even though discounted for the time value of money, than the present investment being made. It is this expectation of greater value in the future that underlies the concept of financial brand value. It's the ability of brand communication to change or reinforce profitable customer and consumer behavior— not attitude change—that really matters.

The calculation of either the royalty rate or the discounted cash flow/net present value is beyond the scope of this text. If we wandered off into that, you'd quickly accuse us of being brand babblers ourselves. All you really need to know is how the financial value of the brand is being determined. And, the two primary ways are estimated royalty rates or discounted future cash flows to determine net present values. Your financial advisor can take you through the details if you really need to know.

If you can handle these two concepts, you can quickly identify the brand babblers and separate them from the brand builders.

Why You Should Spend Money on Your Brand

The key point in all this discussion of brand equity and brand value is, of course, that your brand can grow and prosper and generate future income flows in only four ways:

1. Get more customers for the brand: Increase the actual cash flows coming in now and in the future.
2. Get current customers to buy more or use more or pay more for the brand: Retain or increase the flows of income from current customers.
3. Get present customers to continue to buy the brand for longer periods of time: Increase the length of time the income flow comes into your firm.
4. Get customers to shift their purchases among your portfolio of brands and not wander off into someone else's brand's income flow. This simply means you might get customers to trade-up, cross-buy or add-on products and services that will increase your cash flows over time.

The key ingredient in this approach is that you identify the goals for your brand communication investments in advance. Then, you measure against those goals. Again, the key elements are investments and returns. That's what really builds brand value for you, the brand owner. Without financial results, the attitudinal dimensions of brand equity are of little value. It's only common sense that positive attitudes are virtually a prerequisite to purchase behavior and in that sense necessary and important. But that's the beginning, not the destination, of a profitable branding program. Positive attitudes toward the brand must translate into profitable behavior to produce greater brand equity.

So, when the babblers start talking about brand equity and brand value, simply ask them which or what combination of these four income streams they are going to influence or manage and how much more they estimate you will probably get back over what you will spend. See if they can fit that into their triangles or hierarchy models.

Unmasking the Brand Budgeting Bugaboo

Hidden here, in one of the last chapters of the book, is the real secret of managing brands and branding. That's brand budgeting.

The most common questions asked by brand owners and requested by board members around the world are the three basic brand questions:

1. How much should we invest in our brand or brands?
2. What level of return will we receive?
3. Over what period of time will those returns occur?

If you have followed this text to this point, the answers to these questions should be relatively clear. It's customers and income flows and investments and returns over time.

Why did it take so long to get here and why have we led you through so much brand information and mis-information to get you to this point? Simple. You have to work your way through the babble to get to the pearls of wisdom. And brand budgeting is one of those pearls.

The simple rule for brand budgeting is to invest in your brands based on what you expect to get back, not what you can afford or what you've always done or what the babblers say you need to buy or to match competition or some other surrogate for financial planning.

The financial determination of brand value is the key to any type of brand budgeting.

In Chapter 11, we showed you a simple model that we called the "closed-loop" concept. There, we suggested that customers were streams of income to the firm. The organization invests against customers and prospects either to acquire new income flows, retain present income flows or to grow the income flows from present customers. Thus, if the company knows the value of a customer or customer group, intelligent decisions can be made about how much to invest in the customers and what the returns might be. That's what closes the loop: customer or prospect valuation, investments in brand communication to influence (i.e., increase) that valuation, then measurement of returns that come from customers and prospects as a result of those investments in brand communication.

You invest in customers with various types of brand and branding activities with the goal of either (a) gaining new income flows from new customers or (b) stabilizing current income flows among existing customers or (c) getting present customers to increase their income flows to the firm or some combination of those returns.

Thus, brand investments are investments in customers, not in brand or media or creative or other brand communication stuff. Customers are the only people who give you back income from your investments. So, budgeting is a simple task. How much can or would or could you invest in a customer to be able to generate a profitable return over time? Figure that out for each of your customer groups and you have your brand budget. Investments and returns. Financial models. Pure and simple.

If, for example, you have a group of customers that are worth $1,000 net to the bottom line and you estimate they will be worth that amount for the next five years, then you could rationally invest $1,000 in brand communication each of those years and still break even on your investment.

If you want to make a profit, you would reduce your investment levels to less than the $1,000 they generate. Of course, you'd have to estimate what the future value of your money would be to account for your present investment levels. That's all discounted cash flows really are.

So, brand budgeting becomes relatively simple. Know the value of customers. Invest in those customers with brand marketing and communication activities. Estimate changes in returns as a result of your investments and . . . "ta dah," you have your brand budget. A daunting task? Not really, but extremely relevant to managing your brands.

With this view of brand budgeting and returns, we are ready to sum up. That's what you'll find in the final chapter.

Notes

1. Tim Ambler, "The Long and the Short View of Marketing Metrics," Presentation at the Marketing Science Institute Conference "Measuring Marketing Productivity: Linking Marketing to Financial Returns": October 3, 2002, Dallas, TX.

15

Future Babble

t_o this point, we have dealt almost entirely with current brand and branding issues that are confusing, confounding, and sometimes simply incomprehensible. Give the brand babblers their due. They have taken brand and branding confusion to new heights.

As we have noted throughout this text, much of this babbling comes in the form of self-promotion, that is, the babbler takes a common branding topic, gives it a new spin, dresses it up in new clothes, heads it off in a new direction, or suggests a new meaning commonly with the express purpose of collecting new and bigger checks from you, the brand owner.

That's what often happens when a topic is new and the ground rules are still being established. Recall what has happened to such areas as total quality management (TQM) and most recently to customer relationship management (CRM). Confounding the concept. Changing the terminology. Extending and expanding basic issues into unrelated areas. All are the common approaches by consultants, gurus, experts, and wanna-bes that simply create what we call brand babble.

Babbling is clearly evident in brands and branding. For example, at this point, there is not even common agreement on the definition of *brand*. Thus, all the babbling. That will likely continue and perhaps even increase in the future.

The wary brand owner or manager must always be on the lookout for these new babblings, for they pop up, are promoted, often capture the fancy of the trade press, unfortunately, and become accepted methodologies, concepts, and rituals, often without much substance or empirical verification.

Yet, there are some important issues brand owners and managers must face in the coming years. To provide some direction, five of what we believe are and will be the major branding topics are listed below. Each of these must be addressed if the field is to move beyond the babbling stage.

While our list is in some level of priority and relationship, most likely they will develop and expand at different rates since all are important.

Brand Development #1—Brands and Branding at the Board Room Level

For too long, brands and branding have been the purview of middle managers, i.e., so-called brand managers or even marketing directors. The problem, of course, is that in this type of structure, one of the primary corporate assets, albeit an intangible one, is often being managed as a short-term initiative, typically for the current fiscal year and too many times, for a 90-day reporting period. Middle managers with career aspirations are more inclined to go for the quick hit that shows an immediate spike on a sales report or P&L and leave the long-term wreckage for their successors to deal with.

Brands are too valuable for that type of attention and direction.

Brands, as major corporate assets, must be managed for the long term. That requires senior management and board level attention and initiatives. Therefore, if the organization is to succeed in building its branding capabilities, the brand and its management must move up the ladder to the board level. Senior management hasn't abdicated the control of capital expenditures to middle managers. The same case must be made for one of the firm's most valuable assets, the brand.

Simply put, brands and branding must receive the same attention as capital expenditures, mergers and acquisitions, and compensation plans. Obviously, that will require a more brand-educated management team and a more informed board, but both will be critical if the brand is to grow and prosper and ultimately drive revenues and profits for the owners.

Brand Development #2—Customer-Centric Organizational Structures

Most organizations reflect a manufacturing-age organizational structure and orientation—vertical silos, managed separately and independently by inward looking and generally internally oriented managers. Brands, however, as discussed in Chapter 3, are relationships between the brand owners and the brand customers. Thus, the organization must have a customer focus if its branding programs are to prosper.

Reorienting the organization to becoming customer-centric or at least customer-aware will require a better-informed senior management team and directorial board. (See #1, Brand Development). No matter what or how this is done, most likely the organization will require change in two areas: (a) organizational structure and (b) compensation. It is simply impossible to be customer-focused and still reward employees for flogging products to make quarterly goals. And, it is difficult, if not impossible for vertically-oriented, silo-ed managers who report upward to senior managers to give much consideration to customers or customer income flows when their long-term livelihood depends on this quarter's numbers. Both those issues will have to be addressed if brand ownership is to be maximized in the future.

Brand Development #3—Combine All Knowledge Sources of the Firm

Today, brands are too often managed either through the use of attitudinal data (i.e., how people feel, understand, relate, think about, and so on about the brand) or behavioral data (how they behave toward the brand—i.e., purchases, loyalty, share of requirements, and so on). In other words, when it comes to brand management, most organizations are divided into two camps: feelings and doings. That's the core of the problem: fully understanding and managing brands requires combining and using both types of data. That's going to require new types of research and data gathering.

The most critical issue will be the requirement of more dialog and less monologue with customers and prospects so that their needs and wishes are included in brand development. There is little question that brands, to succeed, are going to require greater cooperation between the buyer and the seller, in short, reciprocity (see Chapter 3). It is here that it has become important for the firm to understand what values it can generate for customers and what values customers believe the brand generates for them.

Brand Development #4—Better Metrics for Brand Measurement

As has been pointed out throughout this book, measurement of brand value, no matter at what level or from what viewpoint, must be improved. The organization invests substantial financial resources into the brand through communication activities and programs. It simply must have some way to determine the return on those investments, certainly more stable financial measures than are currently available.

It will be difficult, if not impossible for senior management to take brands and branding seriously unless and until the metrics for brand measurement are improved and, typically, that means financial measures. The attitudinal side of the branding equation is fairly well developed. The behavioral and quantitative and financial areas need the most work. That means new models, new approaches, and new methodologies. Not just re-habs and re-hashes of time-worn and often irrelevant approaches that were invented for a marketplace that no longer exists. Some of the needed concepts are found in this book, but others will be needed. We simply can't manage the substantial value that brands involve with irrelevant brand babbling from the grandstand.

Brand Development #5—Internal Branding and Support

Over the past several years, most of the brand and branding emphasis has been focused on customers and consumers. That's as it should be. They are the ones who provide the income flows that

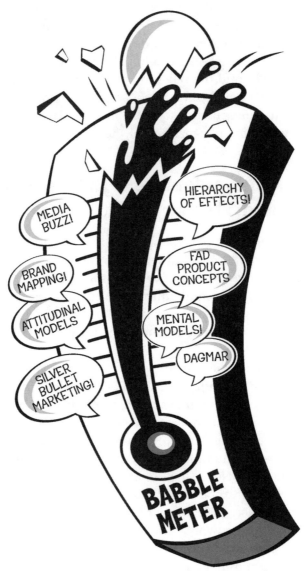

David Metzger

The "Sure-Fire" Approach to Measuring Brand Babble

keep the brand viable in the marketplace. But, increasingly, we are beginning to understand how employees, channels, associates, and other stakeholders at all levels impact and influence the present and future value of the brand and the firm. We know, for example, that the experience a customer has with the brand over time—that is, a consistently pleasant experience—has much greater impact than any type or form of marketing or marketing communication. Thus, it is critical for the management of the brand to understand how these vitally important "brand contacts" and "brand impressions" can be involved, related, and tied to the overall success of the brand.

It is here, in internal brands and branding, that much of the future research, development, and implementation of brand methodologies must occur. That, unfortunately, provides a fertile ground for more brand babbling to develop as well. So, while we must invent and adapt, we must make sure those adaptations and inventions are relevant, consistent, and well grounded. No more brand babble is needed.

With these views of what the future will likely hold for brands and branding, we close this text. We hope our slicing through some of the brand babble has helped you put the entire topic into a better perspective. If nothing else, it should assist you in knowing the questions to ask of the babblers and when to turn on your own personal "babble-meter" to sort the value from the value-less.

Index